FIFTY
FASHION
LOOKS
THAT
CHANGED
THE
1960s

**DESIGN
MUSEUM**

FIFTY
FASHION
LOOKS
THAT
CHANGED
THE
1960s

**PAULA
REED**

THE
1960s

6   Introduction

8   Dusty Springfield 1960
10   Jean Seberg 1960
12   Jean Shrimpton 1960
14   *La dolce vita* 1960
16   Sandie Shaw 1960
18   Audrey Hepburn 1961
20   Kenneth Battelle 1961
22   Diana Vreeland 1962
24   Jeanne Moreau 1962
26   Christine Keeler 1963
28   Elizabeth Taylor as Cleopatra 1963
30   André Courrèges 1964
32   David Bailey 1964
34   Rudi Gernreich's topless swimsuit 1964
36   Vidal Sassoon 1964
38   Bridget Riley 1965
40   Edie Sedgwick 1965
42   Julie Christie 1965
44   Nico 1965
46   The Romantic Look 1965
48   *Blow-Up* 1966
50   *Nova* 1966
52   Emilio Pucci 1966
54   Richard Avedon 1966
56   Truman Capote's Black and White Ball 1966
58   Rive Gauche 1966

Faye Dunaway's sultry looks as the criminal-cum-celebrity Bonnie Parker in the 1967 movie *Bonnie and Clyde* launched a 60s fashion for berets and Depression-era bobs.

Above: Celia's Birtwell's romantic floral prints captured the 'back to nature' mood of the decade.
Below: The 1960s was London's decade and the face of the 'swinging' capital was the model and actress Jean Shrimpton.

60	Anita Pallenberg c. 1967
62	Catherine Deneuve in *Belle de Jour* 1967
64	Faye Dunaway in *Bonnie and Clyde* 1967
66	Granny Takes a Trip 1967
68	Jackie Kennedy 1967
70	Le Smoking 1967
72	Marimekko 1967
74	Mary Quant 1967
76	Penelope Tree 1967
78	Psychedelia 1967
80	Twiggy 1967
82	Ashram style 1968
84	Ossie Clark and Celia Birtwell 1968
86	Marsha Hunt 1968
88	Missoni 1968
90	Valentino 1968
92	Veruschka 1968
94	Talitha Getty 1969
96	Jane Birkin 1969
98	Janis Joplin 1969
100	Jean Muir 1969
102	John Lennon and Yoko Ono 1969
104	Marianne Faithfull 1969
106	Safari Jacket 1969
108	Index
111	Credits

THE 1960s

London defined the spirit of the 1960s like no other city in the world. For one glorious decade, even the couture salons of Paris were in thrall to the energy that was generated in the British capital. It was the city of opportunity, buoyed up by the iconoclastic enthusiasm of its youth.

Britain emerged from the turbulent years of the 1950s a changed country. 'In that period,' wrote American journalist John Crosby, in the *Daily Telegraph* colour supplement, 'youth captured this ancient island and took command in a country where youth had always before been kept properly in its place. Suddenly the young own the town.'

The new social order was unrecognizable to the old guard. As the Duchess of Westminster lamented ruefully to *Vogue*, 'London Society is a world which for better or worse no longer exists.'

In America, the young President and his wife inspired a new idealism. The charismatic Mrs Kennedy, 'eschewed the bun fight and the honky-tonk of American politics and is inclined to the gentler practice of painting, literature and fashion,' said *Vogue*.

In the cinema, long queues formed for the works of stars of the Nouvelle Vague such as Chabrol and Godard, while the pop art movement propelled the likes of Hockney and Warhol to cult hero status. And at the Edinburgh Festival in 1960 Kenneth Tynan remarked, 'England is complacent and the young are bored. There is the desire to hear breaking glass.'

For a decade the world sat back and watched the fireworks.

Bold, bright colours were a 60s leitmotif, capturing the decade's optimistic, freewheeling spirit. Here the models wear chiffon designs by Marc Bohan for Dior. Below: Antonioni's cult film *Blow-Up* (1966) both satirized and celebrated fashionable London. Its emblematic character was a fashion photographer, played by David Hemmings, who thinks he may have witnessed a murder through his camera.

DUSTY SPRINGFIELD

Queen of the Mods

Mary O' Brien (1939–99) was born with a voice that would make her Britain's greatest female pop singer, but everything else that went into the making the icon of Dusty Springfield was her own work. Her career started as part of a wholesome family folk group called The Springfields. A tomboy who was always at the heart of rough-and-tumble play in the dirt, she earned the nickname 'Dusty'.

In 1963, inspired by the music of American girl groups, she went solo. She left the wholesome Springfields behind, ditched her spectacles and embarked on a reinvention that would make her 'Queen of the Mods'. She became the Dusty known the world around in style as well as in name.

Her signature style was carefully crafted, using glittering evening gowns, heavy black mascara, panda eye make-up and huge peroxide-blonde bouffant hairdos. Derek Wadsworth, who arranged a lot of her material in the studio, said, 'It was like putting a jigsaw together. Dusty would have made a great scientist because she analysed every detail. Dusty Springfield was a creation of Mary O'Brien. She was almost not like a real person. She put the whole package together – the hair, the shoes, the gestures – and she had impeccable taste.'

Dusty borrowed elements of her look from the blonde glamour queens of the 1950s, such as Brigitte Bardot and Catherine Deneuve, and pasted them together just the way she liked them. She practised the way Peggy Lee put her eyes on one side halfway through a song and did a little smile. She invented a character the public loved, a face worthy of magazine covers and the breathy speaking voice of a giggly girl next door.

In spite of serial hits, she owned up to desperate insecurity: 'To be the star they wanted, I had to hide behind a mask, and I chose mascara.'

Dusty Springfield's artistic impact is often eclipsed by the glamorous excess of that towering beehive and panda eye make-up. They made her an icon of camp, and inspire catwalk comebacks to this day. But the quality of her voice transcends trends.

JEAN SEBERG

A preppy in Paris

Jean Seberg (1938–79) had already starred in dozens of Hollywood films before moving to Paris. Savage reviews of her work by the critics at home prompted her to seek success in Europe.

Ironically, it was her American preppy style, passed though the filter of French chic, that ended up creating the stereotype of the French gamine. She is remembered for her simple, sporty style that created a fashion look out of such unprepossessing pieces as an oversized man's shirt and ballet slippers. It was also in Paris that she got the famous pixie haircut for which she is most remembered.

At 17 and a complete unknown, she had starred in the Hollywood director Otto Preminger's epic *Saint Joan* (1957). But it was her role in Jean-Luc Godard's directorial debut *Breathless*, opposite Jean-Paul Belmondo, that became her most famous. The image of Seberg as Patricia Franchini strolling down the Champs-Elysées in the *New York Herald Tribune* T-shirt made style news around the globe. And the image still resonates today. In 2010, on the fiftieth anniversary of the release of *Breathless*, Kate and Laura Mulleavy, the sisters behind the California cult label Rodarte, designed a T-shirt featuring the classic masthead that paid homage to the Seberg original. It sold out in days.

Other wardrobe classics for which we have to be eternally grateful to Seberg as Franchini include nautical striped T-shirts, the trilby hat, trench coats, oversized sunglasses, skinny pants and ballet pumps.

Jean Seberg's gamine crop continues to inspire actresses from Carey Mulligan to Michelle Williams. And Jean-Paul Belmondo still sets the standard for smoky French sex appeal. For fashion fans over the years, her newspaper seller's T-shirt is an evergreen style headline.

JEAN SHRIMPTON

'The London Look'

Jean Shrimpton (1942–) was the first high-fashion model also to be a popular pin-up. Her freewheeling style made it possible for a whole world of girls of her own age to connect with the elegant and expensive clothes she modelled. A graduate of the Lucie Clayton College, she was first spotted by David Bailey. As a couple, the pair became emblems of London in the early 1960s. He said it was almost impossible to take a bad picture of her and that even in her passport picture she looked a great beauty. She later dumped him for actor Terence Stamp, but ultimately rejected the glittering celebrity lifestyle at the height of her career for a life in the country.

Shrimpton was always sanguine about fame, and told an interviewer in *About Town* magazine in 1962, 'I am not a classical beauty. Nor a beatnik really, but I am riding the crest of a wave. In a year everyone might be against my type of looks.'

In spite of her modesty, Shrimpton was a household name by the time she was 25. She is also credited with changing the course of popular fashion. The miniskirt may have been born on the catwalk but Shrimpton's appearance in a minidress at the Melbourne Cup in Australia ensured that every woman wanted one. It came about quite by accident when Colin Rolfe, her dressmaker, found he didn't have enough fabric to finish the four outfits she wanted and cut them all above the knee.

Shrimpton was a totem for British fashion. British *Vogue* said: 'The world suddenly wants to copy the way we look. In New York it's the "London Look". In Paris it's "le style anglais". Every kind of English girl seems now to have the self-assurance that praise and admiration gives. Every girl is an individualist, a leader.' 'The Shrimp' was that girl.

Within months, David Bailey's camera turned Shrimpton, a mild-mannered country girl who hated to be stared at, into a sex icon as desirable as Monroe, Taylor or Bardot. For the first time, thanks to her, fashion pages were torn out to become pin-ups in bars and garages.

LA DOLCE VITA

The 'sweet life' with film, fashion and Fiat 500s

No film captured so vividly the flash-bulb brilliance of Italy's postwar *miracolo economico* than Federico Fellini's 1960 masterpiece *La Dolce Vita*. After the miseries of war and fascism, the nation revelled in a consumer boom driven by film, fashion and Fiat 500s. Since then, Rome has never quite separated itself from the fantasy of the 'sweet life'.

Rome of the 1950s had become an outpost of Hollywood, attracting many American productions. Films such as *Ben Hur* (1958) and *Cleopatra* (1963) were shot at Cinecittà, Rome's film studios, renowned as 'Hollywood on the Tiber'. The restaurants were full of American actors, producers and directors, together with the ever-present pressmen and women who followed them around. Indeed, Paparazzo, the ubiquitous news photographer in Fellini's film would give his name to the job.

Fellini brilliantly captured the atmosphere of postwar plenty and excess. To the ordinary men and women of the time, it must indeed have seemed as if the social elite were on a non-stop party circuit. With blithe disregard for schedules and apparently living only for leisurely nights, actors, aristocrats, playboys, dandies, and fashionable intellectuals alike squandered time and resources as if there were no limits. But beneath the glittering surface, *La Dolce Vita* also probes the crisis of a society in transformation, struggling to come to terms with volatile values in an age of mass communication and consumption.

The *New York Times* praised Fellini for his 'brilliantly graphic estimation of a whole swath of society in sad decay' and his 'withering commentary on the tragedy of the over-civilized'. *La Dolce Vita* was the box-office hit of 1960, and launched Marcello Mastroianni as an international heart-throb. In London the release of every Fellini, Godard and Antonioni film was welcomed with long lines at the ticket offices, and together they had a profound influence on British directors and the birth of British neo-realism.

Anita Ekberg, fooling around with Marcello Mastroianni in the Trevi Fountain, created one of the most memorable scenes of modern cinema. On that March evening in 1959, cinematic legend has it that Mastroianni was so cold he needed a wetsuit and a bottle of vodka. It is also reported that Ms Ekberg managed to complete the scene unaided.

SANDIE SHAW

The barefoot diva from Dagenham

1960

'The biggest star ever' – a grandiose claim, perhaps, but back in the mid-1960s, when the Beatles were still very young indeed, Sandie Shaw (1947–) was pretty much the biggest pop star ever – within UK shores, at least.

A 17-year-old sprite with knockout cheekbones and a gorgeous Vidal Sassoon bob, she came seemingly from nowhere (actually Dagenham) to be the first woman to have three number-one hits and the first Briton to win the Eurovision Song Contest. More importantly, she managed, with her fey, barefoot performance style, to transform herself into an emblem of the countercultural spirit of the 1960s.

You might speak of her in the same breath as the other pop poppets of her era – Lulu, Cilla and Petula – but she was, and remains, a much edgier customer. Her break came in the early 1960s when she came second in the Ilford Palais talent contest. It led to an audition in London and an offer to sing at a charity concert in Hammersmith, where she met Adam Faith. Shaw went to number one in 1964 with the Burt Bacharach song '(There's) Always Something There to Remind Me'.

Shaw lived the 1960s dream, sneaking out from under her father's watchful eye to party with Jimi Hendrix, though never for very long, so busy was her work schedule. The original Brit girl, she was the picture of an independent girl about town. To the girls back home in Dagenham it must have seemed as if she had everything: a number one hit record at 17, a fur coat (which she wore during winter and summer) and a white Mercedes. Her record company celebrated her birthday with a cake topped with her famous feet made out of icecream.

When she married fashion designer Jeff Banks in 1967, she was so famous that in order to give her adoring fans and the ever present press the slip, she went to the registry office in disguise.

Sandie Shaw first took her shoes off during the recording session for 'As Long as You're Happy, Baby'. Her manager was nonplussed but Adam Faith reassured him: 'Don't worry, she knows what she's doing.' The public loved it. She believed she sang better barefoot, and ever since has always performed without shoes.

After 1961 and *Breakfast at Tiffany's* there was a veritable army of Audrey Hepburns scurrying around in black evening dresses. The movie's influence was so pervasive that the American Society for the Prevention of Cruelty to Animals reported an avalanche of requests for orange tabby cats. Cats aside, it marked the moment when the Audrey-Givenchy partnership blossomed, as Holly Golightly's hangover chic caused a run on triple-strand faux-pearl necklaces, sleeveless dresses and oversized dark glasses.

The persona Audrey Hepburn consistently projected was one of chic sophistication that was never brittle or cold. But until this point she had specialized in the role of the ingénue; the moment when she first appears in the film on an empty Fifth Avenue still ranks as one of the great screen transformations of all time. *Silver Screen* magazine commented: 'She's changing Hollywood's taste in girls. From the full bosomed, sweater-filling type with more curves than The New York Central Railroad to the lean umbrella-shaped variety.'

There on Fifth Avenue, in her tiara-trimmed up-do, Givenchy gown and evening gloves, sipping from a cardboard cup and munching a danish pastry, Hepburn broke hearts of audiences around the world.

When Truman Capote sold the movie rights of his novella to Paramount, he had wanted Marilyn Monroe to play Holly and complained that Hepburn was 'just wrong for the part.' Director Blake Edwards took a barrage of criticism from the serious cinema reviewers for his 'mawkish' interpretation. There were much higher expectations for leading man George Peppard who was thought to be the next James Dean. But ever since, fashion editors have analysed, models have channeled and women all over the world have copied and aspired to Audrey Hepburn's effortless elegance in *Breakfast at Tiffany's*.

Even now, the online movie site Rotten Tomatoes gives *Breakfast at Tiffany's* an 88-per-cent 'Fresh' rating, concluding: 'It contains some ugly anachronisms, but [director] Blake Edwards is at his funniest in this iconic classic, and Audrey Hepburn absolutely lights up the screen.'

KENNETH BATTELLE

Haute coiffure

No one knew who did Mamie Eisenhower's hair, but everyone knew who did Jackie's – Mr Kenneth. Kenneth Battelle (1927–) was the first celebrity hairdresser; he was also the first hairdresser who was commonly known simply by his first name.

Battelle became a legend in the 1960s thanks to his famous clients who often called on him to perform minor miracles. He managed to transform Marilyn Monroe's permed and over-bleached hair into a kittenish, candy floss halo. His salon on East 54th Street was the epitome of uptown glamour, designed by the celebrated interior designer Billy Baldwin. Customers were highly likely to find themselves in the backwash next to the likes of Lauren Bacall or Audrey Hepburn, as well as the A-list of America's social register.

During the early 1960s, Battelle went from being an insider secret to being a household name when he became known as Mrs Kennedy's hairdresser. He created the tousled bouffant style for Jackie to balance her wide cheekbones and to add height to her slim frame and broad shoulders. Legend has it that he set her hair in specially designed Lucite rollers before combing it out. Millions of women around the world copied her look.

He may have been a trusted member of the First Lady's style team, but in 1962 he also styled Marilyn Monroe's hair for JFK's 45th birthday rally: the night she silenced Madison Square Garden with her infamous rendition of 'Happy Birthday, Mr President'). Less than a year later he cut Jacqueline Kennedy's hair the morning before she left with her husband for Dallas, where he was assassinated.

Arguably, the uptown New York hair salon known simply as Kenneth should have followed mid-century swank spots such as The Stork Club and El Morocco into obscurity. But Mr Kenneth managed to turn it into an institution, and the salon is still tending to the locks of a new generation of party-pages luminaries.

DIANA VREELAND

Fashioning the fashion editor

Having been fashion editor of *Harper's Bazaar* during the postwar years, Diana Vreeland (1903–89) became editor of American *Vogue* in 1962, a tenure that lasted only nine years but which changed magazines forever. She was the original 'High Priestess of Fashion'.

Vreeland positively feasted on the energy and the new styles of the decade. Her imagination fed on the activities of the young, and for many of them she played an important mentoring role. Many influential designers and editors have named Diana Vreeland as an inspiration for their careers.

Her words were powerful and influential. She christened the new trends, along with the people who made them, with the catchy headlines and memorable metaphors for which she was famous. *Vogue*'s use of the term 'beautiful people' became a byword for the chic, rich lifestyle of the 1960s. And, to this day, the portmanteau 'Youthquake' sums up the creative vibrancy of the decade.

Many of her favourite photographers, including David Bailey, Irving Penn and William Klein, are considered to have done their best work with her at this time. Her favourite models redefined the image of modern beauty. To the likes of Veruschka, Marisa Berenson, Twiggy and Jean Shrimpton she gave a free hand to construct their fantasies (or in the case of Penelope Tree – one of her discoveries – her 'fantas-trees'). She commented: 'a little bit of romance, a bit of splendour, a little luxe in our lives … it's what we all crave, yes?'

Open to everything that was new, different and wild, Mrs Vreeland's imagination and her acquisitive eye for the near future encouraged and defined the spirit of exaggeration that was in the air. She promoted the Space Age look of Courrèges with the same enthusiasm as she had the classic fashion of Balenciaga: for her they carried the same message of vitality and excitement.

Richard Avedon said of Vreeland: 'Diana invented the fashion editor. Before her it was just society ladies putting hats on other society ladies.'

There are so many Vreeland 'stories' that she has become almost a mythical character. As Marc Jacobs said, 'Diana Vreeland became both the archetype and stereotype of what it means to be a fashion editor. No one has ever been like her.'

JEANNE MOREAU

The face of the Nouvelle Vague

Jeanne Moreau (1928–) is the Nouvelle Vague incarnate. The film critic Ginette Vincendeau has defined her quality as 'beautiful, but in a kind of natural way; sexy, but intellectual at the same time, a kind of cerebral sexuality.' With her sultry glamour and dry, no-nonsense humour, Moreau became an icon for the fresh new face of French cinema, pioneered by the likes of Godard and Truffaut.

Moreau first drew attention in 1962, when François Truffaut directed her in the part of the mercurial Catherine in what is his undoubted masterpiece, *Jules et Jim*. Truffaut wrote of her: 'Her qualities as an actress and as a woman made Catherine real, made her plausible, crazy, possessive, passionate, but above all adorable.' *Jules et Jim* took numerous prizes worldwide, was a commercial success and confirmed Moreau as a major actress. Her portrayal of a woman who lives for the moment and who goes where her passions lead her was a clarion call for a new generation of liberated women.

That Moreau's look in the movie became an instant fashion hit confirmed another dimension of her powerful influence. Women everywhere were suddenly wearing grandmother specs, long scarves, gaiters, boots, knickerbockers and poor boy hats. Her style influence endured, sending yet more women on the road to ringletted and ruffled romanticism after she made the look famous in *Viva Maria!* (1965), in which she played opposite Brigitte Bardot.

It was at this time that Jeanne met the designer Pierre Cardin. She was trying on one of his outfits and it was love at first sight. They spent five years together, their relationship captured by the press in exotic locations such as Greece and Tahiti or at home in Paris. She became his best-known model and he became the man behind her look. They were one of the most talked-about couples of their time, with the question of whether they would ever marry a frequent subject of speculation. (They never did.)

It was her performance as the alternately coquettish and commanding Catherine in Truffaut's masterpiece, *Jules et Jim*, that made Moreau a star and defined her as an intellectual sex symbol. But she also worked with luminaries such as Buñuel, Antonioni and Orson Welles, who once called her 'the greatest actress in the world'.

CHRISTINE KEELER

The scandalous siren of the Sexual Revolution

Christine Keeler (1942–) was only 16 when she met Stephen Ward. She came from grinding poverty in Berkshire, running away to London to work as a topless dancer in London. The 46-year-old Ward, a society osteopath by day, had a sideline introducing female companions to his well-born friends. Her affair with the Minister for War John Profumo brought down the government of Harold Macmillan, and caused a scandal that reverberated to the heart of the Kremlin.

Keeler paid the price for challenging society's moral code. She might have been a pariah at the time, but is now more generally viewed as the victim of an embarrassed and vengeful Establishment. With the protagonists safely out of the way, the political class were able to draw a veil over the whole nasty affair. Sex was now on everyone's lips, and the press had discovered that it could, and would, expose the private lives of public figures. With her dark, starlet looks, Keeler was also photogenic tabloid fodder. You could say the modern age began here.

As hemlines went up in the 60s, inhibitions came down. Christine Keeler's life reflects the evolution of a new society, one in which working-class youth – hitherto people with few choices about where to go and what to do in life – was suddenly confronted with multiple opportunities. Keeler was collateral damage in the social and political upheaval that not only defined the decade but also changed the world.

The 1989 movie *Scandal*, starring Joanne Whalley, introduced Christine Keeler's story to a new generation. The Profumo Affair gave rise to the type of no-holds-barred tabloid journalism for which Britain is now world-famous and from which no public figure is safe.

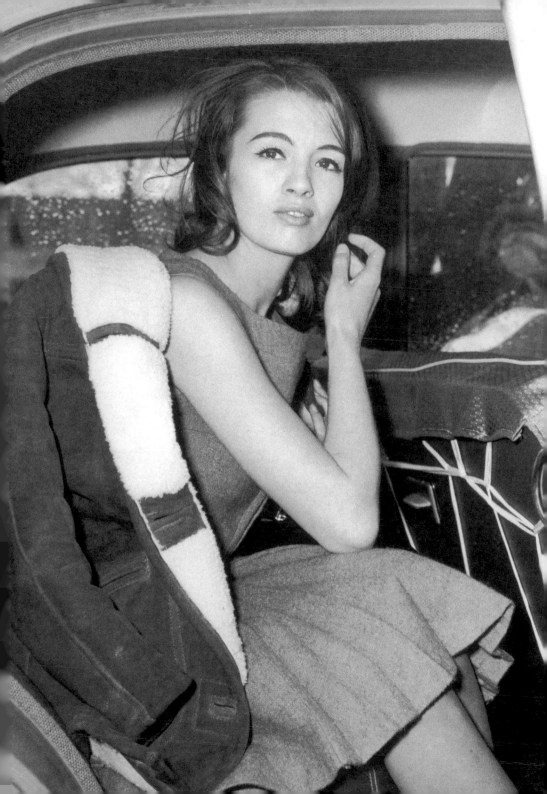

ELIZABETH TAYLOR AS CLEOPATRA

1963

The queen who nearly sank Twentieth Century-Fox

At the time when she took on the role of Cleopatra, Elizabeth Taylor (1932– 2011) was at the very height of her fame as an actress. Many beautiful and powerful female stars had gone before and came after her, but none have fascinated in quite the same way. A startling beauty, Taylor achieved global fame as a child star. Her background (she was born in London to American parents) afforded her a unique transatlantic status – she was both British national treasure and American royalty.

The most famous scene from the 1963 movie is perhaps the defining image of Elizabeth Taylor's epic cinematic career. Cleopatra's arrival in Rome – featuring costumes of 24-carat gold, a cast of thousands and a budget that dwarfed (by almost threefold) the most expensive production that had gone before, nearly sank Twentieth Century-Fox. Every prop and set was built life-sized. A replica Roman forum constructed for this scene was, according to the publicist, 'bigger than the original and about a hundred times as expensive'. The gold-beaded wig she wore to meet Caesar was sold shortly after her death for $11,000.

Nobody loved diamonds quite like Liz Taylor, and few possessed as many. Her collection was the stuff of legend, and in 2011 its sale at Christie's raised $137.2 million. As Taylor remarked, 'Undeniably, one of the biggest advantages to working on *Cleopatra* in Rome was Bulgari's nice little shop.'

It was the highest-grossing film of its year and yet *Cleopatra* still ran at a loss. The enduring appeal of Elizabeth Taylor as the Egyptian queen continues to inspire reinterpretations in the fashion world, not least by Kim Kardashian, who gave it her best shot in the March 2011 issue of US *Harper's Bazaar*.

ANDRE COURRÈGES
A designer for the Space Age

Born in 1923, André Courrèges (1923–) graduated as an engineer at the age of 25. In 1950 he went to Paris to work at the fashion house of Jeanne Lafaurie, before securing a position at Balenciaga. He worked for the couture master for ten years, honing his skills in the cut and construction of garments. In 1961, with his mentor's blessing, he left to set up his own house.

His look was radically different not only from that of Balenciaga, but also from just about everything that was going on in contemporary fashion. His wife and partner Coqueline organized the presentation of his collections, which she conceived explicitly as 'a show', energized by loud music and dancing young models.

His spring 1964 collection, with its linear minidresses and futuristic tailoring, confounded the experts. The look was created using heavyweight fabrics such as gabardine that held a stiff, uncompromising shape. Moreover, he used materials hitherto unheard of in the couture atelier: metal, plastic and a cutting-edge innovation called PVC. Many of the outfits had cut-out panels, exposing backs, waists and midriffs, and shockingly they were also often worn without a bra.

Accessories included flat boots, goggles and helmets inspired by the equipment used by astronauts. With his stark shapes and white and metallic colourways, Courrèges was celebrated as the designer of the Space Age.

From the perspective of publicity, the collection was an absolute sensation. British *Vogue* declared 1964 'the year of Courrèges'. His clothes represented a couture version of the 'Youthquake'-driven street style, and heralded the arrival of the 'moon girl' look. His career may have been short-lived but his influence was seismic. Courrèges made trousers acceptable daywear for fashionable women, and to this day he vies with Mary Quant for the credit of being the inventor of the miniskirt.

Among the whackiest items in Courrège's fashion legacy are a glow-in-the-dark dress and barely-there swimsuits held together only by lacing up the sides. However, high-street retailers loved him. In 1964 the market was awash with plastic skirts and jackets, crash helmets, go-go boots and goggles.

DAVID BAILEY
Sexing up the 60s

A new band of photography stars emerged in the 1960s who hung out with the celebrities they photographed and became just as famous. It was they who propelled the creation of the Swinging London of the decade. David Bailey (1938–) was at the forefront of the group. From humble beginnings, Bailey's prestige sprang from his talent. He commented: 'I had a choice, aged 16. I could either be a jazz musician, an actor or a car thief. They said I couldn't be a fashion photographer because I didn't have my head in a cloud of chiffon. They forgot about one thing. I loved to look at women.'

The US journalist Tom Wolfe noted the cultural sea change: 'Once it was power that created high style, but now high style comes from low places.' Bailey projected his own youth and sexiness through his work. His images had an engaging and uncompromising toughness: black and white, minimalist and very graphic. 'I've always hated silly pictures and gimmicks,' he has said recently. With a small single-lens reflex camera he was freed from the constrictions of tripod and studio, and was just as likely to snap high fashion in the street as in an exotic location.

Bailey was every bit as interested in being part of the new style as he was in recording it. He dressed to suit his image and became a cult hero. When he married Catherine Deneuve in 1965, his best man was Mick Jagger. The event caused a media storm. In 1966 the movie *Blow-Up* concerned itself with the work and sexual adventures of a London fashion photographer who was largely based on Bailey.

David Bailey walked into *Vogue* in the summer of 1960 and changed fashion pictures into portraits full of sexual tension. He battled the fashion establishment in order to make his mark, and to this day remains one of the most distinguished British photographers.

RUDI GERNREICH'S TOPLESS SWIMSUIT

Scandalizing the American public

Rudi Gernreich (1922–85) was the darling of the American avant-garde. Courrèges and Quant might have been showing the shortest skirts, but Gernreich went one step further and presented a topless dress which made headlines (though not many sales).

He also made the monokini, a topless swimsuit that was worn by Peggy Moffit, his favourite model. The skimpy garment might have chimed with the scantily clad sunbathers on European beaches, but it was banned in the US. The American public were scandalized. Throughout the country, statesmen and church officials pronounced the swimsuit immoral and tasteless.

Many people assumed the monokini was meant to be nothing more than a fashion stunt. However, despite the reaction of critics and churchmen, shoppers purchased it in unexpected numbers that summer. By the end of the season, Gernreich had sold 3,000 swimsuits at $24 a pop (a tidy profit for such a minuscule amount of fabric). Still, despite the number of swimsuits that were bought, fashion history records that very few monokinis seem to have ever been worn in public.

Gernreich is credited with other fashion firsts. His design goal was to perfect a slim body line with seaming and no darts, and, as the perfect foundation garment, he created the 'No-Bra' with cups made from triangles of sheer nylon net attached to shoulder straps and a narrow elastic band encircling the ribcage. He took the heavy inner construction out of bathing suits. He created early body stockings and leggings based on dancers' leotards and tights but using flesh-coloured mesh and black jersey. He experimented with an androgynous look by putting men in skirts, and was an early adopter of the use of heavy metal zips as decoration.

Gernreich, an enthusiastic nudist, became notorious with his topless swimsuit design. The mayor of San Francisco declared, 'Topless is at the bottom of porn.' In Russia it was dismissed as a 'sign of social decay'.

VIDAL SASSOON

Revolutionizing hairdressing with the five-point cut

Vidal Sassoon (1928–2012) made celebrity hair history when he was paid $5,000 to cut Mia Farrow's hair for her role in *Rosemary's Baby* (1968). At the time of the world-famous haircut Mia was married to Frank Sinatra, and media buzz sometimes blamed the demise of her marriage on her shockingly short pixie Sassoon cut. Whether it was true or not, it seasoned the fame of Sassoon.

It was his mother who helped the young Vidal land his first hairdressing apprenticeship in an East End salon, where he began to develop an appreciation of geometry. Sassoon had early dreams of being an architect before joining the Israeli Defense Forces in 1948, but his architectural approach to hair eventually made him the most sought-after hairdresser of the 1960s.

Sassoon cuts were all high fashion and low maintenance. Before him it was all roller sets and 'hair-dressing'. Sassoon created shapes that were so modern and so forward-thinking that they still look 'modern' nearly 50 years later. His lasting contributions include the five-point cut worn by fashion designer Mary Quant, and Nancy Kwan's angular bob in *The World of Suzie Wong* (1960). Alongside Quant, Sassoon 'styled' the 1960s. As the fashion designer herself says, 'I made the clothes, but he put the top on.'

The hairstyles relied on dark, straight and shiny hair, precision-cut into shape. His geometric haircuts might have looked severely cut, but they were wash-and-go and entirely lacquer-free, relying on the natural shine of the hair for impact.

Sassoon was a key force in the commercial development of hairstyling, and built his worldwide empire by putting together a team of super-talented hairdressers. The 'architecture of the face' always guided his thinking, and he found constant inspiration in the work of the Bauhaus architects and designers. He considered it one of his greatest achievments when scholars of the German modernist school later recognized the Sassoon cuts as 'part of the forward movement of design'.

Vidal Sassoon admitted that his success owed much to Mary Quant, who came to him with a conundrum: 'Vidal, I am sick to death of all these chignons. Surely there is another way to keep the hair off the clothes.' Sassoon replied: 'Sure, you could cut the whole damn lot off.'

BRIDGET RILEY

Mesmerizing a decade with op art

The British artist Bridget Riley (1931–) was a reluctant fashion icon. In New York in 1965, for the opening of her highly anticipated Museum of Modern Art exhibition 'The Responsive Eye', she was horrified to see dresses with designs lifted from her paintings in the Madison Avenue shop window displays. She was incensed by the way her art was being 'vulgarized in the rag trade'. She even tried to sue an American clothing manufacturer who had produced a line of dresses inspired by one of her paintings: a piece of her work that he had bought for his own collection.

But Riley was fighting a losing battle. Her breakthrough had come as the explosion of 1960s youth culture gained momentum. Works such as *Blaze 1* (1962) and *White Discs 2* (1964) – whose hypnotic black-and-white patterns gave the impression of swelling or warping movement – synthesized the hallucinogenic mood of the times. British fashion manufacturers found untold applications for Reily's artwork. Shopping bags, car bodies, paper napkins and furnishing fabrics were among some of the items produced in her monochrome motifs that most exasperated the artist.

If Riley thought she could ride out the passing Mod fad at home, she was mistaken, as when The Who arrived in the US she was discovered by a whole new audience who considered her work an essential part of the London Look. Riley went global, although perhaps not in quite the way she would have liked. In spite of her objections Bridget Riley became one of the most influential people in the fashion world.

The fashion, design and advertising industries fell in love with op art's graphic patterns and mesmerizing, decorative impact. Across all design disciplines op art was cool, and Bridget Riley (shown here in a photograph by Tony Evans) became Great Britain's number-one art celebrity.

EDIE SEDGWICK

Poor little rich girl: Queen of The Factory

In 1965, at the age of 22, Edith ('Edie') Sedgwick (1943–71) met Andy Warhol at a party in New York. An heiress from a dysfunctional Californian family, the gamine bottle-blonde with cropped hair, kohl eyeliner and antique chandelier earrings captivated Warhol. Before the night was out he had cast her in *Vinyl* (1965), the movie he was making.

Punk-rock legend Patti Smith recalled: 'She was such a strong image that I thought, "That's it." It represented everything to me, radiating intelligence, speed, being connected with the moment.' Sedgwick became 'Queen of The Factory', the New York studio where the Warhol inner circle worked and partied. She was the antithesis of the society heiress of the time, and fascinated in her long dresses and bare feet, accessorized with her grandmother's jewels. Her opaque tights, leotards, false eyelashes and shoulder-grazing earrings inspired Edie-wannabes everywhere.

For a short time Warhol and Sedgwick were inseparable. She dyed her hair silver like his. He wore a striped jumper to match hers. By 1966 Sedgwick was no longer just a cult figure. She modelled for *Vogue*, who described her as 'white-haired with anthracite-black eyes and legs to swoon over'.

Ultimately, her relationship with Warhol was short-lived, but her style and image influenced a whole generation and continue to inspire – from Kate Moss's cropped haircut in 2001 to Sienna Miller's interpretation in the 2006 movie *Factory Girl*, and John Galliano's 2005 show for Christian Dior. Galliano cited her as an influence, saying, 'She may only have had 15 minutes of fame but her style and image influenced a whole generation.'

For a woman with no discernible talent, Edie Sedgwick made a huge and lasting impact. Bob Dylan's 'Just Like a Woman', 'Leopard Skin Pillbox Hat' and 'Like a Rolling Stone' are all purportedly about Sedgwick. In 2006 Sienna Miller played her in the film *Factory Girl*.

JULIE CHRISTIE

Fashion drama on the frozen steppes

The British actress Julie Christie (1941–) made a huge impact with a passing appearance in *Billy Liar* in 1963, and was immediately catapulted to *Vogue* style status. The fashion magazine called her a 'kooky blonde' and 'one of the best things in the film'. She quickly became a star in her own right, and shot to superstardom with her roles in *Dr Zhivago* (1965) and *Far from the Madding Crowd* (1967).

As the impossibly beautiful Lara in *Dr Zhivago*, she made the maxi coat a fashion must-have overnight. Few films have had a comparable influence on fashion. With the 60s in full swing the miniskirt had far from run its course, and yet John Fairchild, publisher of *Women's Wear Daily*, waged a personal crusade to drop hemlines after developing a fashion crush on Lara's wardrobe. Indeed, Christie's role ranks among the few that continue to inspire fashion designers to this day.

In *Dr Zhivago* director David Lean championed his leading lady, carefully lighting her face and placing her in breathtaking locations and costumes. The epic tale of love in a war-torn Russia divided by revolution and ideology uses clothes to express the theme of social change. Thus Christie's elegant aristocratic wardrobe of the early part of the film gives way to sober military uniform. Inevitably military tailoring also caught the popular imagination.

In 1967 *Time* magazine observed: 'What Julie Christie wears has more real impact on fashion than all of the clothes of the ten best-dressed women combined.' By this time Christie was a superstar who commanded $400,000 a movie.

Phyllis Dalton won an Oscar for her costumes in *Dr Zhivago,* but remembers the demands of director David Lean who was concerned with every detail: 'He made all his actors wear period undergarments beneath all their costumes for added authenticity, even though they were never visible in any of the film's scenes.'

Counterculture femme fatale

Nico (1938–88) is best known as a member of the original Velvet Underground, and was a key player in the legend created around them by Andy Warhol. But even before those heady New York City days, Nico had enjoyed considerable success as a model and actress. Living in Paris at the beginning of the 1960s, she graced the pages of a number of iconic fashion magazines. And, while working as a model, she had also landed a part in *La Dolce Vita*, sung on a soundtrack composed by Serge Gainsbourg and had a child with Alain Delon.

Nico was born in Cologne, and her father was killed in action during World War II. She was discovered by a photographer in Berlin, became a model in Paris and then in 1965 the Rolling Stones guitarist Brian Jones introduced her to Andy Warhol in London. She looked him up again when she went to New York in 1966, as a model under contract to Eileen Ford.

Warhol remembered meeting her: 'She was sitting at a table with a pitcher in front of her, dipping her long beautiful fingers into the sangria, lifting out slices of wine-soaked oranges. When she saw us, she tilted her head to the side and brushed her hair back with her other hand and said very slowly, "I only like the fooood that flooooats in the wiiine."'

With her eye-skimming fringe and pale-blonde hair, Nico created her own distinctive look in slim-cut mannish tailoring. When Warhol began managing the Velvet Underground he proposed they take on Nico as singer. She sang lead vocals on three songs ('Femme Fatale', 'All Tomorrow's Parties', 'I'll be Your Mirror') on the band's debut album, *The Velvet Underground and Nico* (1967), one of the most legendary rock albums of all time.

Nico (seen here in the white suit) was a pin-up for the man's trouser suit as an effortlessly chic piece of clothing. The style icons' style icon, Chloë Sevigny, admits she has pictures of her on her walls. And she is cited as inspiration by musicians from Bauhaus and Marc Almond to Siouxsie Sioux and Björk.

THE ROMANTIC LOOK
Fashion reconnects with its softer side

'In fashion the revolution is over. A new quiet reigns.' So said *Vogue* in 1967, ushering in an era of exotic romance.

There was a marked change in direction from futurist to nostalgic fashion; from minimal to baroque; from hi-tech to handmade. In reaction to the uniformity of geometric haircuts and 'functional' fashion, stiff, carved tweed suits and creaking plastic, women wanted to dress up and look wild and beautiful. For evening wear, pure theatre came in the form of brilliant colour, lavish prints, rich embroidery and tall boots, imagined to be the staples of wardrobes in gypsy camps all over the Ukraine.

The movement had three style tribes. The youngest was the 'flower power' school (think Pattie Boyd with her Native American fringed suede, headbands and colour-clashing layers of crêpe and brocade). It was a kind of dressing-up-box style with tassels, fringes, bows and bells. Then there was the Mayfair version: a jet-set rendition of picturesque poverty that favoured ethnic gypsy dresses, Indian pantaloons, Afghan coats mixed with sheepskin and gold embroidery. In London, 'Indian' and 'Middle Eastern' boutiques sprang up everywhere.

The third tribe was the ruffle-and-ringlet lot inspired by the movie *Viva Maria!* (1965), starring Brigitte Bardot and Jeanne Moreau. This favoured a daytime look of velvet knee-breeches and men's suits with ruffled shirts, and for evening long, demure dresses in fragile fabrics, frilled and tucked bodices, milkmaid sleeves, bib fronts and lace edgings. The hair was worn in ringlets or shoulder-length curls and tied in bunches of ribbons. Or it was left loose in Pre-Raphaelite waves and Ophelia ripples, with eyes painted icing green or harebell blue. London's King's Road looked like a Russian ballet, and 1920s beaded dresses became treasured pieces.

As *Vogue* concluded in 1969, 'the pop revolution burns out with a crackle of paper dresses'.

Ruffles and ringlets in the retro romp *Viva Maria!* became a huge hit thanks to Bardot and Moreau. Only in the 60s could a movie succeed as part epic Western, part sex comedy, part slapstick, part Marxist tract. Moreau and Bardot shone as women who invented striptease and led a Central American revolution.

BLOW-UP

A snapshot of Swinging London

Director Michelangelo Antonioni's first English-language film was a sensation. It tells the story of a fashion photographer's accidental involvement with a murder and captures the atmosphere of Swinging London – from the hip parties, peopled with reefer-smoking dudes, to the gangs of earnest student mime artists let loose on the streets. Every bit as important as super-snapper Thomas and his dolly girls is the stylish world they inhabit: a world of fast cars, glossy magazines and rock 'n' roll.

The film features David Hemmings (as Thomas), Vanessa Redgrave and Sarah Miles. Jane Birkin made her name in the movie playing 'the blonde'. One of the most famous models of the day, Veruschka, has a cameo in a scene in the photographer's studio, which *Premiere* called 'the sexiest cinematic moment in history'. Veruschka's writhing body, under Hemmings' close-quarters camerawork and breathless urgings, has also been mimicked and lampooned countless times ever since.

Plot aside, *Blow-Up* marks the historical moment when the partnership of photographer and model achieved popular cult status. The fashion industry was spawning stars to equal screen idols. The photographer Thomas is generally considered to have been inspired by David Bailey, but there is more than a hint of Terence Donovan in him, as well as a smattering of John Cowan (in whose studio the movie was in part shot).

Another notable cameo was by the Yardbirds, who perform 'Stroll On'. Jeff Beck, playing alongside Jimmy Page, smashes his guitar over an amplifier in an obvious nod to The Who, a band who had been invited to appear in the film but refused.

Antonioni turns an outsider's eye on a London that was just beginning to swing, and captures the moment. But a film intended as an attack on a certain type of modern sophistication ended up celebrating the fashion and music of the very world it set out to criticize.

NOVA
Redefining women in print

In the late 1960s, *Nova* magazine was Britain's 'style bible' and a ground-breaking women's magazine. Launched in 1965, it arrived at the perfect time to chart and document the evolution and fallout of the 'Youthquake'. There was so much to talk about. Mary Quant had revolutionized wardrobes. Rock 'n' roll was one of Britain's most successful exports. The pirate radio station Radio Caroline was making waves in the conventional music media. And more and more people had a television, which brought world politics and culture into the home.

The iconic *Sunday Times Magazine* which employed established as well as emerging photographic talent had started publishing articles on fashion, lifestyle and interior decoration. *Nova* settled into the niche inhabited by intelligent women who wanted more from their magazine than simply fashion and cookery. It would be another six years before *Cosmopolitan* arrived with its no holds barred agenda of sex and celebrity, and another twenty before *Elle*.

Nova was the first of its kind; a politically radical, unashamedly controversial and fearless in the pursuit of intelligent opinion. Its agenda ranged from sex and the pill to feminism, homosexuality and racism. There were 5,000 word articles by Christopher Booker, Susan Sontag, Irma Kurtz and photographs by Helmut Newton and Don McCullin. Its fashion editors, Molly Parkin and Caroline Baker, had a massive impact on the fashion of the era.

After a meteoric rise *Nova* fell victim to aggressive competition and closed in 1975 after only 10 years in operation.

Nova challenged everyone's idea of what a women's magazine should be, embracing risk and taking chances in features and photography. *Nova* epitomized the concept of the avant-garde and reshaped the scope of women's publications forever.

EMILIO PUCCI
The irresistible lure of colour

Nineteen-sixties' psychedelia found high-fashion expression in the radiant prints of Emilio Pucci (1914–92). His slinky silks in vibrant swirling patterns became a wardrobe staple of the jet set. His daring juxtaposition of acid yellows, lime greens, Aegean turquoises and fuchsia pinks became a distinctive design signature, recognized the world over to this day.

A dashing Florentine aristocrat, Pucci made his fashion debut quite by accident. In 1947 a ski suit that he designed for a friend was spotted on the slopes of Zermatt in Switzerland, and was subsequently featured in the pages of *Harper's Bazaar*. Thus began his career as a designer of sport and resort clothes. His social connections gave him a guaranteed entrée into the beau monde, and soon everyone from Sophia Loren to Jackie Kennedy was sporting his iridescent creations. Marilyn Monroe was even buried in one of his dresses. The Pucci trademarks spoke of colourful ease: sexy narrow-legged pants, easy tunic tops and loose blouses.

In 1965, a New York ad agency was hired by Braniff International Airways to update its image. Pucci was commissioned to design new clothes for the hostesses. The advertising tagline read: 'The End of the Plain Plane'. The uniforms so captured the public imagination that Barbie had all four versions in her wardrobe. Among the more unusual innovations was a 'bubble helmet' – a clear plastic hood worn by flight attendants between terminal building and aircraft to protect their hairdos from the rain and the blast of the jet engines.

Imagine the joy of the jet-set traveller: to discover not only that could she fit dozens of Pucci outfits into a single bag, but also that they emerged wrinkle-free. In the sybaritic 60s, this simple practicality contributed enormously to Emilio Pucci's overnight success.

RICHARD AVEDON

The man who turned fashion
photography into art

When director Stanley Donen went looking for inspiration for the elegant fashion photographer played by Fred Astaire in his movie, *Funny Face*, he looked no further than Richard Avedon. In a decade when fashion photographers were as famous as rock stars, Richard Avedon was the poster boy for his profession.

A high-school dropout, Avedon learned the rudiments of photography as a merchant marine in the 40s. In 1945 he got his first break at *Harper's Bazaar*. 'I was overwhelmed. Mrs Vreeland kept calling me Aberdeen and asking me if a wedding dress didn't make me want to cry. They are all serious, hard-working people. They just speak a different language. So I took my models out on the beach and photographed them barefoot, running, playing leapfrog.' The experiment was a hit and he became a staff photographer at *Harper's Bazaar*. Working alongside Alexey Brodovitch and Diana Vreeland, he evolved a style that was rich in narrative, energy and movement.

Central to *Harper Bazaar*'s appeal were the outdoor shoots and innovative photography, and Avedon was one of the magazine's stars. His style reverberates through the work of contemporary photographers such as Steven Meisel and David Sims, and anyone else who directs a model to stride or leap across a seamless background, or attempts to capture her in an unobserved private moment. Twiggy (see page 80), who had a relatively short career, is the poster girl of the 1960s largely because of his pictures of her.

While shooting the Paris collections for *Bazaar*, Avedon would take the clothes out of the salon and onto the street. He invented scenes and storylines for models like Dovima and Dorian Leigh, or his first wife, Doe Avedon. Avedon's minimalist aesthetic and athletic power helped create some of the most memorable fashion images of the decade. He was the 60s frenetic energy in human form. As his friend and fellow fashion photographer Lillian Bassman once said, 'Did you ever meet Dick? He was always jumping around.'

In 1965 Avedon left *Bazaar* and followed his close ally Diana Vreeland to *Vogue*. In total, their collaboration would span 40 years.

Avedon's photographic style has been widely imitated by photographers across the decades. Generations of models have leapt across white backdrops, struck an athletic attitude in a blank set or simply sat lost in thought in a café — all on account of Richard Avedon.

TRUMAN CAPOTE'S BLACK AND WHITE BALL

1966

The night the writer made 500 friends
and 15,000 enemies

When the author Truman Capote threw a lavish ball to celebrate
the phenomenal success of his 'nonfiction novel' *In Cold Blood*, he
conjured a way to make it the most talked-about party of the decade.
He would invite his friends, who included the most famous people
in the world. He would request they all wear black or white. And he
would have them hide their fabulous and much-photographed faces
behind masks.

'They rolled off the assembly line like dolls,' wrote Enid Nemy in
the *New York Times*, 'newly painted and freshly coiffed, packaged
in silk, satin and jewels and addressed to Truman Capote, the Plaza
Hotel.' CBS dedicated a special programme to the arrivals. Viewers
at home were rapt. 'This is how the other half lives,' quipped the
announcer before continuing archly, 'We know you were not rich,
social, or beautiful enough to be invited, or you wouldn't be up
watching the news.' He added, 'the "Henrys" are here, Ford and
Fonda … but not the "Edwards" …', meaning the Duke of Windsor
and Kennedy, who had both rsvp-ed 'non'.

Frank Sinatra came with Mia Farrow, who incited rumours of
pregnancy by wearing an empire-line dress and mutterings of
curiosity by showing off the new gamine crop she had chosen for
the role in *Rosemary's Baby*. Tallulah Bankhead, Babe Paley and
Gloria Guinness were belles of the ball. Lauren Bacall danced with
the choreographer Jerome Robbins 'in a fashion', Truman Capote
noted, 'that Fred Astaire and Ginger Rogers might have envied'.
Jackie Kennedy's sister, Lee Radziwill, had to sit the dancing out
in case beads from her gown showered the dance floor.

Women wore multiple hairpieces, teased, tamed and twisted
by the hands of Kenneth Battelle – known as 'The Mr Cool of the
Haute Coiffure'. Leo Lerman told the *Life* photographer Henry
Grossman that he 'had never seen so many beautiful women in
one place at one time'.

Breakfast at Tiffany's
catapulted Truman Capote
to a level of stardom that few
writers reach. *In Cold Blood*
– his laconic account of a
notorious quadruple murder
– created a wave of acclaim
and controversy that would
carry him for years to come.
But some say the Masked
Black and White Ball was truly
one of his greatest works.

RIVE GAUCHE
YSL offers power to the people

In 1962, Yves Saint Laurent (1936–2008) left Dior, and on 29 January of that year the Yves Saint Laurent couture collection made its début. *Life* magazine called it 'the best collection of suits since Chanel'.

Saint Laurent's reputation was built on his supreme tailoring. The first to feminize a man's tuxedo, with 'Le Smoking' in 1966, he anticipated power-dressing by a decade. The Saint Laurent jacket became a symbol of success for career women throughout the world. The designer also knew that high fashion needed the energy of popular youth culture to inject new verve into its stale atmosphere, so he frequently visited London during the 60s to find inspiration in the boutiques of the King's Road.

By the mid-1960s, although London was in full swing, Paris was still putting couture on a pedestal. In 1966, Yves Saint Laurent and his partner, the industrialist Pierre Bergé, were the first among the French fashion establishment to turn away from the rarefied couture ateliers to the relative accessibility of prêt-à-porter. From the early years of their business partnership, Pierre Bergé was astute enough to know that although couture equalled kudos, it was the glamorous accoutrements – perfume, accessories and cosmetics – that would turn YSL into an international force. It was Bergé who urged Saint Laurent to do ready-to-wear, and in 1967 the house opened a prêt-à-porter boutique – Rive Gauche (Left Bank) – in a former bakery at 21, rue de Tournon.

A pioneer in his day, Saint Laurent was the not only the first to popularize ready-to-wear fashion; he also broke the social taboo on trousers for women, and was the first designer to include black models in his runway shows. Pierre Bergé, who remained Yves Saint Laurent's close friend and business partner until the designer's death, has said that while Chanel gave women freedom, Yves Saint Laurent gave them power.

Barely five years after founding his couture house, Saint Laurent explained his prêt-à-porter project simply: 'I want to break away from the idea that haute couture is the sole image of fashion. Fashion is what can be worn. This is the main square, not a closed circle.'

ANITA PALLENBERG

'Evil glamour'

Born in 1944, Anita Pallenberg grew up in Rome and went to a German boarding school. Keith Richards famously said that when he first met her he was almost overwhelmed: 'She knew everything and she could say it in five languages. She scared the pants off me.'

Expelled from school at 16, Anita Pallenberg graduated to the upper echelons of cool. She first made her way to Rome to hang out with the *dolce vita* crowd, and then in New York with the Andy Warhol crowd, before moving to Paris to begin working as a model. In 1965 she met the Rolling Stones at a concert in Munich.

Brian Jones was the first to fall for what Marianne Faithfull called Pallenberg's 'evil glamour'. But a passion for mod fashion and the mysteries of the occult were not enough to sustain a relationship that was tempestuous and often violent. In 1967 she ran off with Keith Richards while the band was on holiday in Morocco.

Pallenberg made a living as an actress. Her credits include *Barbarella* (Keith offered her £20,000 not to do it, but she did it anyway) and *Performance* (the backdrop for an alleged affair with co-star Mick Jagger and her first encounter with heroin). 'Anita is a Rolling Stone,' said Jo Bergman, the band's one-time assistant. 'Her influence has been profound. She keeps things crazy.'

Pallenberg and Richards had two children before the band's lawyers urged a split. What followed were decades of addiction and notoriety. She once spent a month at the Grosvenor House Hotel in London without ever leaving her room, and claims to remember nothing of an occasion when a 17-year-old boy shot himself in her bedroom.

She remains a notoriously glamorous figure, a kohl-eyed icon whose style has influenced the likes of Kate Moss and Sienna Miller.

Whenever a girl dons a shaggy fur coat, velvet pants, floral minidress, floaty tunic and shorts, tops it off with a wide-brimmed hat and works that 'I'm with the band' vibe, she should remember, she owes it all to Anita Pallenberg: the mother of all rock chicks.

CATHERINE DENEUVE IN *BELLE DE JOUR*

Chaste eroticism and French chic

In 1968 the critic Frances Wyndham dubbed Catherine Deneuve (1943–) 'a cool combination of the virginal and the vicious'. It was her portrayal of an icy, sexually adventurous housewife in Luis Buñuel's 1967 *Belle de Jour* that established her as one of the most compelling actresses of her generation, and Yves Saint Laurent as one of the most influential designers. The movie marked the beginning of what would be one of fashion's most significant partnerships, for it was here that the actress and designer first met. To this day, the YSL costumes that Deneuve wore in the film are continually referenced in fashion and pop culture.

Deneuve plays Séverine, a doctor's wife who leads a double life. A prostitute by day, turning her fantasies into reality, she becomes a housewife by night, when she settles into prim domesticity with her husband. The Saint Laurent wardrobe plays a supporting role that speaks volumes about her character. In tailored coats and dresses, she is the perfect Parisienne. In the brothel, in lingerie and silk, she becomes the confident seductress.

Saint Laurent had a decades-long relationship with Deneuve, and it would be alongside his muse that he took his bow at his very last show. It has been said that their relationship never advanced much beyond formal terms, but together their fashion influence has enjoyed an enduring incandescence.

'Saint Laurent designs for women with a double life,' Deneuve once said. 'His clothes for daywear help a woman to enter a world full of strangers. They enable her to go wherever she wants without arousing unwelcome attention, thanks to their somehow masculine quality. However, for the evening, when she may choose her company, he makes her seductive.'

Referencing the power of the actress's quiet elegance, Saint Laurent dismissed the more extreme designs of the day: 'It pains me physically to see a woman victimized, rendered pathetic, by fashion.'

Director Luis Buñuel cared less for Deneuve's nakedness than for the clothes that covered it in his fetishistic movie *Belle de Jour*. It's her glazed and highly polished feminine surface that takes centre stage, and her YSL wardrobe that plays the greatest supporting role.

FAYE DUNAWAY IN
BONNIE AND CLYDE
The death of the mini

'They are young, they are in love, they kill people.'

Originally conceived as a stark black-and-white film about the notorious Texas outlaws, with a look based on the Dust Bowl-era photographs of Walker Evans, *Bonnie and Clyde* became a box-office hit in 1967 and a trendsetter for the decade. It was something entirely different: less neo-realist, more stylish folk ballad. The movie presented its murderous couple as romanticized and immensely attractive nonconformists. It was a portrayal that chimed with young 1960s audiences, who strongly identified with the fugitive lovers.

Theadora Van Runkle's costumes had a massive impact on the world of international fashion, though she had struggled to get her ideas accepted. Faye Dunaway (1941–) had originally wanted to wear slacks as Bonnie Parker, since she realized that the character would need to move freely to race in and out of getaway cars. Theadora, however, went with a more glamorous wardrobe, with long skirts, a beret and a short jacket. And the 'Bonnie and Clyde Look' became a fashion rage.

Bonnie's outfits were fluid and looked as though they could be packed fast should the wearer need to go on the lam. They were feminine but suffused with a tomboy sexuality. Van Runkle remembered Ms Dunaway needed to be convinced. 'Faye thought I didn't care how she looked,' Ms Van Runkle told a fashion critic. 'She thought I was trying to make her ugly.'

It is no exaggeration to say that Dunaway's wardrobe as Bonnie Parker triggered the death of the mini and ushered in the midi.

The film became a catalyst for a revival of ladylike chic across the US: berets and bobs were the quintessential headwear, while longer pencil skirts were rediscovered by the mini-wearing youth, creating a new breed of femme fatale.

GRANNY TAKES A TRIP

The new face of fashion retailing

In the long history of retailing, Granny Takes a Trip was a mere blip that lasted only four years. But the little shop that opened in 1965 at 488 King's Road changed everything. The originators were the journalist Nigel Waymouth and his girlfriend Sheila Cohen, who intended to sell Sheila's collection of vintage clothes. The arrival of the Savile Row tailor John Pearse set the project off on a swirling, theatrical, psychedelic trajectory with enough creative energy to make London the shopping mecca of the world.

London's main shopping attraction of the day, Carnaby Street, was the hub of an early kind of fast fashion, pioneered by the queen of that scene, Mary Quant. Granny Takes a Trip launched the King's Road as an alternative destination. And there were rich pickings on the secondhand market for the lavishly embroidered Savile Row uniforms that had become redundant in 1939 when men were no longer required to wear formal court dress. Anything braided, tailored, tassled and swaggerworthy was becoming standard issue for any self respecting rock god. The eclectic vintage collection of original Victorian and Edwardian clothing, sold alongside Pearse's Savile Row tailoring, launched a boho chic that, to this day remains an assuredly London look.

Behind a series of surreal (and temporary) shopfronts, Granny Takes a Trip peddled a mysterious and exotic glamour. It was like a grown-up dressing-up box in which psychedelic fantasy and fin-de-siècle romance collided. Among the first customers were the Beatles and the Rolling Stones, who wore Granny's clothes on the album sleeves of *Revolver* and *Between the Buttons*. Jimi Hendrix, Ossie Clark, Anita Pallenberg, Brigitte Bardot and Andy Warhol hung out there, too.

Within three months the shop was featured in *Time* magazine, which was celebrating the arrival of Swinging London, and a few weeks later the team rang the changes with the first overhaul. Out went art nouveau and in came two giant and forbidding images of Native American chiefs, Low Dog and Kicking Bear, rendered as psychedelic portraits.

Granny's triggered the boutique boom and influenced the dozens of stores that followed in its wake. The original Granny's team went their separate ways in 1969.

Granny Takes a Trip transformed the way fashion and clothes were sold. A 'psychedellic art project' that became a mecca on the hippie prilgrimage, it sold a brand of renegade fashion that did exactly what it said on the tin.

JACKIE KENNEDY

Fashion's first lady

Jacqueline Kennedy (1929–94) was 31 when she became First Lady, a role that had been filled for the previous 64 years by women old enough to be her mother. After generations of matronly First Ladies, Jackie Kennedy gave the American public what they never knew they needed – glamour. Kennedy radiated enviable qualities – confidence, independence and intelligence. Well-bred and properly educated, she was the walking definition of class. She set a new example of how young American women ought to be.

The French-born but naturalized American Oleg Cassini was her first official designer, a choice that stunned the experts who had assumed her choice would be America's leading designer, Norman Norell. But it was a smart move by the 33-year-old, who was addicted to French couture but was nonetheless obliged to show the electorate that she bought American.

Early on, *Women's Wear Daily* – the US fashion bible – implied that Jackie had been smuggling French couture clothes into the White House. And when the President and Mrs Kennedy went to France, another guest at an Elysée reception discovered she had ordered a dress from Cardin's spring collection that was identical to the Cassini one worn by the First Lady – 'So identical that Paris couture couldn't believe their eyes.' To the industry, the Cassini factor suddenly made sense. She would not so easily have persuaded Norman Norell to knock off his French counterparts. When she made her stunning entrance at the palace of Versailles in a Givenchy gown, all controversy was set aside and WWD dubbed her 'Her Elegance'.

The average American housewife basked in Jackie's motherhood, her refinement and her lofty pursuits, which included riding to hounds and reading Proust. Kennedy was responsible for the mass adoption of styles such as the pillbox hat, the bouffant hairdo, the shift dress and low-heeled pumps.

Jackie was a powerful weapon in the Washington diplomatic armoury. In this picture she is on a visit to Cambodia, which had broken relations with the US in criticism of the Johnson campaign in Vietnam. However, they rolled out the red carpet for the former First Lady and her party. And Prince Sihanouk declared her 'the best ambassadress America could send'.

LE SMOKING
The new little black dress

When Yves Saint Laurent first presented 'Le Smoking' as part of his 'Pop Art' collection there were two versions: a jacket and trousers in grain de poudre with four button-down pockets; and a straight-cut, high-waisted satin version over a white organdie blouse. Both offered an initially controversial alternative to the classic little black dress or evening gown.

At first, editors and buyers didn't get it. *New York Times* critic Gloria Emerson panned the collection. It was, she said, 'lumpy' and 'outdated', arguing that Saint Laurent 'strains too hard to convince the world he is hand-in-hand and eye-to-eye with the very young'. Nonetheless, Le Smoking was instantly sanctioned by a chic collective of style icons including Catherine Deneuve, Betty Catroux, Françoise Hardy, Liza Minnelli, Loulou de La Falaise, Lauren Bacall and Bianca Jagger.

Yves Saint Laurent was seen by many as empowering women by giving them the option to wear clothes that were normally reserved for men of influence and power. Over the next 30 years he reinvented his signature silhouette in hundreds of new and different guises, reissuing it as a dress, short suit and jumpsuit, and for day or evening wear.

Looking back, it's hard to believe that throughout the 1960s, society frowned upon a woman wearing pants outside of her home. Even into the 1970s, very few 'good' restaurants would admit a woman in trousers. La Côte Basque in New York famously turned away YSL devotee Nan Kempner in Le Smoking. In response, she stripped off the pants there and then, and marched into the restaurant wearing only the jacket, re-appropriated as an ultra-short minidress.

'For a woman, Le Smoking is an indispensable garment with which she finds herself continually in fashion, because it is about style, not fashion,' said Saint Laurent. 'Fashions come and go, but style is forever.'

The Winter 1966 collection was not universally well received: proof, perhaps, that critics are not always right. For with the introduction of Le Smoking, Saint Laurent found his definitive muse: the independent woman. The tuxedo would be included in YSL collections for the next 30 years and revolutionized the feminine wardrobe.

'One has to dream. And one must stand out from the rest': this was the famous declaration of the Finnish textile designer Armi Ratia (1912–79), co-founder of Marimekko at the start of her career. In a world mired in postwar malaise, Ratia's playful prints were a shot in the arm for the fashion industry.

The catalyst was the failure of her husband's business venture in an oilcloth factory. The facility was converted into a garment plant instead and Armi asked some artist friends to apply their graphic skills to textiles. In order to show how the fabrics could be used, the company then used them to design a line of simple dresses.

At the very first Marimekko fashion show, held in a hotel in Helsinki, women reportedly 'went wild' for her graphic print shift dresses and they were a sell-out success. Two pioneering designers set the tone for Marimekko: Vuokko Nurmesniemi (1930–) in the 1950s and Maija Isola (1927–2001) in the 1960s. Isola's iconic poppy-print pattern designed in 1964 is a bestseller to this day.

Two key breakthrough moments set the company on the path to its meteoric rise in the 1960s. In 1957 Giorgio Armani, then working as a window dresser for the Italian department store Rinascente, invited Ratia to display her relaxed cotton shift dresses there. And in 1959 Jackie Kennedy bought seven dresses from the then little-known Marimekko brand, and was photographed on the cover of *Sports Illustrated* magazine wearing a loose-fitting sleeveless version in red.

The effect on sales was instant. More casual than what Paris had to offer, the Marimekko look chimed with new attitudes and increasingly relaxed dress codes. During the 1960s the company expanded globally, and became widely known for its casual, often unisex clothing aimed at a young clientele. Accessories and products for the entire home quickly followed.

The Marimekko Corporation in Finland not only sparked a revolution in printmaking, but also pioneered a new definition of fashion that embraced an entire lifestyle.

Idealism and optimism were the driving principles behind Marimekko's exuberant prints (here, the Keidas pattern designed by Annika Rimala). The brightly coloured textiles chimed with the optimism of the decade, and shot to high-fashion status when Jackie Kennedy wore a Marimekko dress on her husband's presidential campaign.

MARY QUANT

The driving force behind democratic fashion

Before the 1960s, the fashion industry was a stuffy institution. Few options were open to young designers. They could set up a boutique, join a couture house (and hope to work their way up) or start a wholesale business. Mary Quant (1934–) was one of the most business-savvy designers of a new generation. With her husband, Alexander Plunket Greene, she rebelled against the traditional bastions. 'We wanted to increase the availability of fun to everyone. We felt that expensive things were almost immoral and the New Look was totally irrelevant to us.'

Quant's King's Road store Bazaar opened in 1955 and was the first boutique to offer cheap clothes designed specifically for the young. She had not intended to make her own clothes, but couldn't find what she wanted among traditional wholesalers. Conventional knitwear companies balked at lengthening a cardigan by 12 inches so she could sell it as a dress. She attended night classes and bought material from Harrods to make stock in her Chelsea bedsit.

Bazaar was a sensation, and lines formed around the block. Her vision of fashion democracy meant that girls and young women could have fashion that was made for them, not watered-down versions of stuff made for countesses and film stars. When the straight-cut shift was shown in Paris in the late 50s, the fashion world was forced to take Bazaar seriously, as Mary Quant had been selling the shape for over a year by that time. By the mid-1960s – it was undoubtedly her decade – Quant's business was worth over a million pounds.

In 1964 Quant spearheaded the introduction of the London Look in the US, reaching thousands of young American girls through J C Penney before the Beatles even made it Stateside. Her models in their thigh-high dresses stopped traffic on Broadway. All over the world, Mary Quant became the byword for contemporary British style.

Many in the fashion establishment hated the attention London was getting. When Chanel was told Mary Quant admired her beyond all others, she replied: 'From her, it is a very small compliment.' 'The amazing thing about being young', said Mary, 'is that — yes — you're scared, but you take it for granted that you can do it. And I did.'

PENELOPE TREE

The 60s It Girl who changed the notion of beauty

For a dazzling and memorable moment at the end of the decade, the 60s belonged to Penelope Tree (1950–). *Vogue* model and muse to David Bailey, she seduced the photographer away from Catherine Deneuve and became the ultimate 60s It Girl. Her eccentric looks and unconventional style would get furious reactions in the streets of New York for her barely-there minis and raccoon-tail skirts.

She was born into a well connected and wealthy family who had plans for her to study English literature at university. That changed when she was spotted aged 17 by the legendary American *Vogue* editor Diana Vreeland at Truman Capote's Black and White Ball. She was wearing a skinny tunic with split seams over thick black tights.

Together with Richard Avedon, Vreeland changed her life. London might have had 'The Twig', but New York had 'The Tree'. 'She's perfect. Don't touch her,' said Avedon to an editor who suggested tweaking her look. Tree relished the possibilities a fashion career offered escaping her conventional background. 'People thought I was a freak. I kind of liked that.' When John Lennon was asked to describe her in three words, he is said to have replied: 'Hot, hot, hot, smart, smart, smart!'

Her relationship with Bailey and her fashion career ended abruptly when late-onset acne left her with scarring. She has recently told Louise France in the *Guardian*: 'I went from being sought-after to being shunned, because nobody could bear to talk about the way I looked.'

According to photographer David Bailey, 'Penelope Tree is the most original model there's ever been. She's the most original-looking girl I've ever seen.' One of the 1960s' elegant survivors, in 2006 she came out of retirement to star in a Burberry ad campaign.

PSYCHEDELIA

Challenging boundaries and breaking rules, with love

Psychedelia was born in the hippie heyday in the Haight-Ashbury district of San Francisco. Style heroes were musicians from psychedelic rock bands, such as the Jimi Hendrix Experience, Pink Floyd and Jefferson Airplane, as well as funk artists such as Sly and the Family Stone, and folk musicians like Bob Dylan and Joni Mitchell. Psychedelic drugs fuelled the audiences at rock concerts and the clothes reflected the buzz of 'tripping out'.

The uniform was instantly recognizable: long hair and luxuriant facial hair for men and hair tied back with headscarves for women; clashing colours and loud textures; bell-bottom trousers, love beads, tie-dye T-shirts and peasant blouses. There was an obsession with just about any non-Western-inspired clothing: cue trends for anything Native American, African, Indian or Latin American. Much of hippie clothing was self-made, in protest against Western consumer culture. The textures and curvilinear shapes of art nouveau were appropriated and mashed up with less romantic imagery from cult comics.

Many white hippies of the 1960s counterculture identified with the American Civil Rights Movement, and those with curly or 'nappy' hair wore their hair in afros in earnest imitation of African Americans. The twin ideals of peace and love governed a lifestyle that encompassed sexual openness, communal living, recreational drug use and a fondness for nudity. Vegetarianism and a proclivity for Eastern religions and fascination with mysticism further separated the 'love children' from the mainstream.

The low-cost utilitarian Volkswagen Bus became counterculture symbol, and many were given flamboyant custom paint jobs. A peace symbol often replaced the VW logo.

The psychedelic hippie movement had only a brief flowering before being appropriated almost immediately by the mass market.

The summer of 1967, with its 'love-ins', 'be-ins', and 'flower power', came to be known as 'The Summer of Love', and was one of the seminal moments of a generation. No boundary, be it in music, fashion, politics, art or literature, was left uncrossed, frequently with the help of mind-expanding drugs.

BILL GRAHAM PRESENTS IN SAN FRANCISCO
THE
TUES. WED. THURS. ONLY
FRI. SAT. SUN. ONLY
THE DOORS
PLUS ALL WEEK
BLUES BAND
TICKETS
SAN FRANCISCO: City Lights Bookstore; S.F. State College (Hut T-1); The Town Squire (1318 Polk); Reilly Galleries (3673 Sacramento); Wild Colors (1418 Haight); Bally Lo (Union Square); BERKELEY: Discount Records; Shakespeare & Co.; SAN MATEO: Town & Country Records; REDWOOD CITY: Redwood House of Music; PALO ALTO: Dana Morgan Music; SAN RAFAEL: Record King; SAUSALITO: The Tides Bookstore

TWIGGY

The world's first teenage supermodel

As a teenage model, Twiggy weighed just six and a half stone. 'Much too thin,' she now says emphatically. 'I had a look – I can see that now – but I don't think I was beautiful. I was a skinny schoolgirl, stuffing tissues into my little 32A bra. I wasn't trying to be that thin, I was perfectly healthy, but still – that look is a total impossibility for women over the age of 20. Fashion has a lot to answer for, doesn't it?' But her body matched Diana Vreeland's description of the perfect contemporary silhouette: 'the smallest calves; the straightest legs; tiny, narrow, supple feet; and beautiful wrists and throat.' Accordingly, Twiggy was an incandescent overnight success.

As with so many romantic rags to riches stories, Twiggy's started with a happy accident. Early in 1966 she had been told that, at 5 feet 6 inches she was too short to be a model. Her only booking had come from Leonard – hairdresser to London's smart set – who wanted to cut her shoulder length hair into a new pixie crop for a shoot to promote his salon.

Barry Lategan's photographs were spotted by the *Daily Express* fashion editor Dierdre McSharry who asked to meet the schoolgirl, and invited her to tea. She arranged to have more pictures taken and, as Twiggy thought, that was the end of it. A few weeks later on 23rd February back home in Neasden, her father woke her up with a copy of the *Daily Express* in his hand that featured a headline announcing 'The Face of 66: The Cockney kid with a face to launch a thousand shapes … and she's only 16!'

Her first glossy magazine shoot was for *Vogue*. Bookings with superstar photographers such as Avedon, Cecil Beaton, Helmut Newton, Guy Bourdin and Norman Parkinson followed and assignments in New York and Paris filled her the diary. Within a year her arrival at international airports was greeted by screaming fans.

By the age of 17, Twiggy was one of the most famous faces on the planet. Her career was a blip by modern standards, lasting only from 1966 to 1970, but it helped define a decade.

ASHRAM STYLE
Spiritual enlightenment, rock-star style

It was the ultimate 1960s scene: the ashram in Rishikesh, India, where in February 1968 the Beatles, Donovan, Mia Farrow (recently divorced from Frank Sinatra) and a Beach Boy or two gathered along the shores of the Ganges, wreathed with marigolds, to meditate at the feet of the Maharishi Mahesh Yogi. The gathering received such frenzied worldwide attention that it is still considered a significant early encounter between Western pop culture and the mystical East.

The ideal of communal living had exploded with a surge of fervent idealism in the mid-1960s. The stereotypical commune was filled with devotees of yoga and vegetarianism, who wore kaftans, Jesus sandals and toe rings, and who practised a lifestyle of free sex and drug use. Young people, it seemed, were looking to escape what they believed was an irreparable society and to build a new one.

The Beatles joined the quest for spiritual enlightenment. For them, it was 'an extraordinary period of creativity' that inspired some of their greatest songs including, 'While My Guitar Gently Weeps', 'Revolution' and many other songs from 'The White Album' (1968). 'Dear Prudence' was written for Mia Farrow's sister, who was so absorbed in her spiritual journey that it was John and George's job to get her to 'come out to play'.

And yet they all came away bitterly disillusioned. Neil Aspinall, The Beatles' road manager, said of the Maharishi: 'This guy knows more about making deals than I do.' Lennon wrote the song 'Maharishi' (with the lines 'What have you done? You made a fool of everyone') as he was leaving. The title and lyrics were soon changed from 'Maharishi' to 'Sexy Sadie'.

The Beatles' ashram experience left an indelible mark on the decade – which is ironic considering just how brief it was. They first met the guru in the late summer of 1967 and by April 1968 it was all over. 'Why?' asked the Maharishi. 'Well, if you're so bloody cosmic, then you'll know, won't you?' Lennon retorted.

The line-up of devotees, wreathed in flowers, at the feet of the Maharishi is a 'who's who' of the 60s music scene: Ringo Starr, Jane Asher, Paul McCartney, George Harrison, Patti Boyd, Cynthia Lennon, John Lennon and the Beach Boys' Mike Love. However, what started as a beautiful thing in 1967 ended in cynical disillusionment in 1968.

OSSIE CLARK AND CELIA BIRTWELL
Romantic femininity

Ossie Clark (1942–96) and Celia Birtwell (1941–) met as students in Manchester in 1959 and married in 1969. Their creative partnership began with their 1966 collection for the chic Chelsea boutique Quorum.

Owner Alice Pollock commissioned a collection of dresses after meeting Ossie at a party. He delivered a collection in white and cream chiffon that sold out immediately. For the follow-up, Pollock suggested he move things along by working in textiles designed by Birtwell. The result was a collection of dresses that invoked the laid-back glamour of the jet set hippie. They were a sell out success. And so began one of fashion's most famous collaborations. This partnership would last for almost all of Clark's career in fashion. Author Judith Watt comments: 'People say that Celia was Ossie's muse, which indeed she was, but their work absolutely went hand in hand. It was her designs that he used to create his.'

About Ossie, Celia Birtwell has said in a recent interview with the *Daily Telegraph*, 'He was a genius, better than Yves Saint Laurent. His cut – although he lifted it from the 1930s, he had his own take on it – even plump women felt pretty in. He didn't dress just the slimmest, which is always easier.' Birtwell's romantic and feminine designs, inspired by Bakst and Matisse, provided the drama to Ossie Clark's cutting patterns. While she was busy in the design studio, he was often out partying with the drug-fuelled Chelsea set. But Ossie's hedonistic style combined with Celia's delicate prints made the pair an unbeatable design team.

Ossie Clark enjoyed meteoric success on both sides of the Atlantic. His was the look of the late 1960s and 1970s. His biographer, Linda Watson, has written that Clark's brilliance was in part a consequence of his bisexuality. 'He understood a woman's body in a way not many men can. He saw them as goddesses – as many gay designers do – but also intimately understood a woman's anatomy. His dresses were sensual, never vulgar or crude. They were man magnets.'

Ossie Clark's flattering cut combined with Celia Birtwell's romantic textiles to produce clothes that are highly prized by collectors to this day. Their glamorous but easy-to-wear dresses anticipated the mood of the hippie years and attracted a glamorous international following.

S41

S39

S37.

S40

S42
F.

S38

2/00
111

MARSHA HUNT
The original 'melting-pot' beauty

In 1969 Patrick Lichfield shot Marsha Hunt (1946–) for British *Vogue*: 'The pictures were supposed to be for the cover,' the model recalled, 'which would have made me the first black woman on the front page of *Vogue*. It didn't happen, but there was a huge spread inside. In those days, it was quite something.' The accompanying text declared: 'People stare at Marsha Hunt on London streets. She knows it. She doesn't mind. Who cares? She's she. She's free.' It also described her as 'London's prettiest golliwog' – a reminder that racial equality and sensitivity were still some way off.

Marsha was the embodiment of black beauty, a woman with a halo of hair. 'The natural' – as the afro was dubbed – was the symbol of the Black Is Beautiful movement, and was as much of a counter-cultural statement as hippies' long hair. Lichfield's image showed her naked – appropriately enough for a London cast member of the musical *Hair*, and became a quintessentially iconic image of the 1960s.

Hunt, had impeccable 60s credentials. She hailed from Philadelphia, the city of brotherly love, studied at Berkeley, and joined Jerry Rubin's anti-Vietnam protest marches. She moved to London in 1966 where she remembered 'anything seemed possible.'

In addition to her (relatively small) role in *Hair*, she signed a recording contract in 1968 with the same company that had The Jimi Hendrix Experience, The Who, Thunderclap Newman and Arthur Brown.

She met Mick Jagger when the Rolling Stones asked Hunt to pose for an ad for 'Honky Tonk Women' (1969), which she refused to do because she 'didn't want to look like [she'd] just been had by all the Rolling Stones'. Jagger took her out and their nine- or ten-month affair began. They had a daughter, Karis, in 1970.

Europeans, Marsha discovered, identified her as an American, not as African-American or black. She herself describes her skin colour as 'oak with a hint of maple', and has said, 'Of the various races I know I comprise—African, American Indian, German Jew and Irish—only one was acknowledged.' Hunt invented her own word to describe herself, a combination of the French word *mélange* (mixture) and melanin: the Melangian.

MISSONI

Masters of the not-so-traditional knit

Ottavio ('Tai') Missoni started in the knitwear business making tracksuits. He met his wife and business partner Rosita, a swimmer, while competing for the Italian team at the 1948 London Olympics. They started their knitwear business in 1953.

By 1958 the Missonis had produced a striped knitted shirtdress, and the crossover from sports to fashion was under way. Initially producing knitwear for other designers, the couple first came to the attention of the fashion world in the mid-1960s, when they created a knitwear collection for the French designer Emmanuelle Khanh. For their own label, however, they pushed the conventional boundaries of knitwear to new and daring limits. Influenced by folk art and design, they started with simple stripes, then graduated to more complex, kaleidoscopic zigzag patterns as their success enabled them to buy more sophisticated equipment. Never again could machine knit be dismissed as boring. In 1965 they got their big media break, with recognition from the influential Italian fashion writer Anna Piaggi.

Collections inspired by silhouettes of the 1920s were global Missoni hits in 1968 and 1969, and the couple became famous for their distinctive style. Their clothes are created from many types of fabrics – wool, cotton, linen, rayon and silk – and, of course, a dazzling array of colours. Their impact was such that, by the early 1970s, the Missonis' allegiance to Milan heralded that city's rise to pre-eminence as a fashion centre.

By the end of the decade and with only a few collections to their name, the Missonis had already snared Diana Vreeland and the mighty *Women's Wear Daily* as allies. *WWD* supported their debut with a dollop of name-making notoriety and the headline, 'Missoni; In the Lead with the Most Sinful Dresses'.

VALENTINO

1968

Couture versus counterculture:
Valentino delivers a decisive blow

In 1959, after serving an apprenticeship at Jean Desses and Guy Laroche in Paris, Valentino Garavani (1932–) opened his own house on Via Condotti in Rome.

Among his first customers was Elizabeth Taylor, who was in Rome with Richard Burton for the shooting of *Cleopatra*. She ordered a white dress to wear to the premiere of *Spartacus*. Numerous international stars from Audrey Hepburn to Rita Hayworth, Italian icons from Sophia Loren to Claudia Cardinale, and glamorous royals such as Princess Margaret were to follow.

In the 1960s the world's fashion focus was on Swinging London, with its boutiques and budget fashion. Valentino specialized in luxury and sought clients who enjoyed a privileged lifestyle that had nothing to do with the street, but he was ready to rise to the challenge. He created a ready-to-wear collection, and in the fashion press at least claimed 1968 as his own. While the fashion world was obsessed with bright colour, he showed white. Vogue wrote: 'Valentino's white – the talk of Europe. And all triumphs for the 35-year-old designer who has become the idol of the young, a new symbol of modern luxury.'

The growth of the counterculture in the 1960s meant that elegant clothes were increasingly seen as an irrelevance. Valentino spent much of the decade swimming against the tide of popular trends. Paris was engulfed by student demonstrations in 1968, when Valentino opened his boutique on avenue Montaigne. But his talent was boosted by his fair share of good luck: in the same year Jackie Kennedy chose Valentino to design her wedding dress for her marriage to Aristotle Onassis, and he became a household name overnight. The designer said, 'I owe so much to Jacqueline Kennedy. She became a very close friend. I designed her entire wardrobe and she made me famous.'

His trademarks were black and white, but he also perfected his own shade of Valentino red, declaring, 'After black and white there is no finer colour.' And his animal prints, including leopard, zebra and giraffe, became timeless classics, yet were immediately identifiable with the start of the decade when fashion began to turn away from street fashion to rediscover luxury.

By 1968, the young Valentino Garavani had already made a name for himself with the red gowns which, to this day, are hallmarks of the house style. But the white collection of the same year was a smash hit, and proved that street fashion could not claim all the fashion limelight.

VERUSCHKA
Fashion's self-styled shape-shifter

Veruschka was born in 1939, the daughter of a German count. Her full name (with title) was Vera Gottliebe Anna Gräfin von Lehndorff-Steinort. Her father was executed after the 1944 assassination attempt on Adolf Hitler, and the family spent the rest of the war in labour camps. She studied art in Hamburg before moving to Florence, where she was discovered by Ugo Mulas, a photographer who was documenting the Italian avant-garde.

Veruschka was a powerful presence in a world of mannequins and quickly became one of Diana Vreeland's favourite models. But at over six feet tall Vera was not showered with offers for commercial work, and with a presence of mind that was decades ahead of its time she set about reinventing herself. Vera became Veruschka, and made the most of her height and Amazonian build. When director Michelangelo Antonioni cast her in his 1966 film *Blow-Up*, she became a star. Her performance may have lasted only five minutes, but her scene with David Hemmings straddling her writhing body is the most memorable of the movie.

After that, it was said she could earn up to $10,000 a day, a fantastical sum at the time. What is certain is that the best photographers in the world were lining up to work with her. But she was ambivalent about being a fashion star: 'I was frustrated very fast about being a model. I think that Diana Vreeland must have sensed it. She introduced me to Franco Rubartelli in Rome. I had the idea that the only way would be to work with a photographer, to have your own ideas and visions about how you wanted to transform yourself.'

Going back to her fine-art roots, Veruschka became a pioneer in the art of body painting and redefined herself again as a 'Creative Futurist'. She collaborated with stylists such as Giorgio di Sant' Angelo, with whom she created an unforgettable fashion story in Arizona equipped only with bolts of cloth, furs and a bag full of wigs.

In October 2010, at the age of 71, she modelled for Giles Deacon at London Fashion Week.

'I was always being different types of women,' admitted the Amazonian mannequin who, at six foot one with size 8 feet, was no standard fashion plate. She busied herself with pushing the boundaries of beauty and became one of the decade's most memorable faces. 'I copied Ursula Andress, Brigitte Bardot, Greta Garbo. Then I got bored so I painted myself as an animal.'

TALITHA GETTY

This photograph of Talitha and John Paul Getty Jr., taken by Patrick Lichfield on a Marrakesh rooftop, is one of the most enduring images of the 1960s. The town had become the ultimate destination for hippies in the late 1960s and the Gettys were some of its most charismatic residents.

As an actress, Talitha Dina Pol's CV extended no further than a bit part in *Barbarella* (1968), but as a fashion icon her style was the embodiment of a certain kind of 60s glamour – a hippie de luxe style that has been reimagined over and over ever since. Everyone from Dries Van Noten to Roberto Cavalli, from Dolce & Gabbana to Matthew Williamson, has paid tribute to her influence with their collections.

When Rudolf Nureyev met her in 1965, he was completely smitten. His biographer Julie Kavanagh speculates that he may have actually fallen in love with an androgynous reflection of himself. Nevertheless, he told friends that it was the first time that he had been erotically stirred by a woman and he wanted to marry her. Talitha passed him over for Getty, the petroleum heir, whom she married in Rome in 1966. She wore a white mink-trimmed minidress for the ceremony.

The couple honeymooned in Marrakesh, where they set up home in the nineteenth-century Palais de la Zahia. Known as the 'Pleasure Palace', their home became infamous for extravagant, drug-fuelled house parties that often included the Beatles and the Rolling Stones among the guests. It was here, too, that she and Yves Saint Laurent became friends. He first visited on holiday and became close to her in 1967, later claiming that 'when I knew Talitha Getty my vision completely changed'. He remembered the couple 'lying on a starlit terrace in Marrakesh, beautiful and damned'.

Talitha Getty was only 30 when she died of an overdose of heroin in 1971, in the same 12-month period that saw the deaths of Jimi Hendrix, Janis Joplin, Edie Sedgwick and Jim Morrison.

Talitha and John Paul Getty Jnr model Moroccan kaftans on the terace of their holiday home in Marrakesh. Photographer Patrick Lichfield was commissioned by American *Vogue*.

JANE BIRKIN

Innocent Lolita or femme fatale?

English-born Jane Birkin (1946–) first gained attention as an actress at the age of 20, when she snagged a minor role in Italian director Michelangelo Antonioni's *Blow-Up* (1966), a controversial film about photography, sex and murder. Birkin played 'the blonde', a leggy model who takes off her clothes and jumps into an awkward 'Swingin' Sixties' sex scene that drew plenty of scandal at the time, but which now seems as campy ridiculous as a clip from an Austin Powers movie.

That same year, she auditioned in France for the lead female role in *Slogan* (1969). Though she did not speak French, she won the role. She co-starred with Serge Gainsbourg and performed with him on the film's theme song, 'La chanson de slogan' – the first of many collaborations between the two. In 1969 she and Gainsbourg released the duet 'Je t'aime … moi non plus' (I love you … me neither), which Gainsbourg originally wrote for Brigitte Bardot. The song caused a scandal for its sexual explicitness, and was banned by radio stations in Italy, Spain and the UK.

Birkin's head-turning fashion choices – her sheer knit minidress and cut-off shorts, as well as her classic trench and sober, low-heeled shoes – cast her as inspiration for any fashionable bohemian. She is loved by designers to this day for her effortless and dishevelled sex appeal: as potent in a glamorous evening dress as in jeans and a tight T shirt.

From her signature straight-cut bangs and stringy brown hair to her almond eyes and mile-long legs, her beauty was a remarkable mix of both innocent Lolita and languorous femme fatale.

At the end of the 60s the world was in thrall to a new type of beauty: the 'leggy soft-skinned blonde in country shoes, classic raincoat and grey flannel'. *Vogue* nominated perfect examples of the type in Jane Fonda, Françoise Hardy and Françoise Dorléac. But first among equals was Jane Birkin.

JANIS JOPLIN
Liberating style

Janis Joplin carved a place for herself as a hard-loving, hard-living red-hot recording and performing star in the male-dominated world of rock 'n' roll. Contemporary critic Richard Goldstein described Joplin's stage presence as 'the total antithesis of the star entrance'. 'Her lumpen extraordinary face has no makeup. Her long brown hair doesn't shine. She screws up her eyes over constant cigarettes and her lubrication and sustenance seem to be sickly Southern Comfort.'

At the University of Texas she was once nominated as the 'ugliest man on campus'. An outcast from her family and her home town, she moved to San Francisco. Her rise was meteoric but her isolation was constant. 'Onstage I make love to 25,000 people,' she said. 'And then I go home alone.'

By 1968 she had become as famous for her idiosyncratic and influential style as for her music. At the Monterey Festival she swapped her sweatshirts for lamé (which she pronounced as 'lame'), lynx and denim plastered with peace symbols. Her signature beads, bangles and feathers were imitated by fans and fellow rockers alike. Sporting a small heart on her breast, she also helped popularize the tattoo. She wore so many long bead necklaces, she joked she didn't need to wear a shirt.

The 1960s rock critic Lillian Roxon credited Janis with helping to liberate American women from girdles and boned bras. At festivals all over America, there were 'the daughters of Janis, their tough and battered little faces defiantly free of makeup and other synthetic improvements.'

The Joplin meteor disappeared in a fiery crash when she died of a heroin overdose in 1970. Her biographer Alice Echols noted she was 'one of the last famous women whose deaths were in some way linked to the irreconcilability of being an artist and a woman'.

With her inimitable style, Joplin influenced fans and fellow rockers alike. She wore feathers through her hair and clothes and made the tattoo cool. Her look, as with the rest of her life, was about excess: in colour, size and shape.

JEAN MUIR
Queen of the dress

1969

Jean Muir (1928–95) served apprenticeships at Liberty and Jaeger before starting her own business, Jane & Jane, in 1962. Before anyone talked of ready-to-wear, she blazed a trail in the fashion business, bridging the gap between mass market and couture. She carved a creative niche with her unique rigour of line and elegance of proportion. Her clothes were meticulously controlled and demure, yet managed to reveal every line of the body. 'I design feminine, not feminist clothes,' pronounced Miss Muir (as she liked to be addressed). 'I like my clothes to be womanly, not fussy.'

In 1966 Muir opened Jean Muir Ltd, and in 1967 a French magazine named her '*La reine de la robe*' (queen of the dress) – a tribute that raised her to the elite coterie that included Vionnet, Mme Grès and Chanel. She preferred the title of dressmaker to that of designer. She called fashion an 'exacting trade' requiring both work and intelligence. 'I love the fittings, getting the shape right. I love the mathematics of it.' Her version of simple reflected an elegant, almost austere persona. She herself wore only navy-blue clothes and her home was decorated entirely in white. She became known for her technical genius and the sheer craft of her work, which was based primarily on cut and meticulous detailing.

A lover of the ballet, Muir favoured fluid fabrics, especially matt jersey, and she used tucks instead of darts to create shape. As a result, the silhouettes had fluidity without sacrificing structure. 'Because I am small I never liked extra weight,' she said. 'I wanted to make clothes that looked like couture but were ready to wear. You had to eliminate a lot.'

Jean Muir believed that women designers were gifted with a common sense that enabled them to make elegant clothes that were also comfortable. 'I think men rather superimpose shapes on women. In today's rather complex world I think a woman has got infinitely more common sense.' Trendless and timeless, she was always more about evolution than revolution.

For her entire career, Jean Muir's design signature was honed with garments that were skilfully tailored and minimally detailed, with long, fluid lines. Favourite fabrics were always jersey, crêpe and suede, usually in dark, plain colours. To her, a fashion trend would have been an anathema. Style was the ultimate goal.

JOHN LENNON AND YOKO ONO

Giving peace a chance

Every generation has its couples who mesmerize the public. In the late 1960s, none felt the worldwide glare of the press more than John Lennon and Yoko Ono. They became the emblematic leaders of a universal cultural revolution.

The Vietnam War was front-page news when they met in 1966, at one of Ono's performance art exhibitions, at the Indica Gallery in London. Having been frustrated in his search for spiritual enlightenment in an ashram, Lennon became fascinated by Ono, whose path to maturity in traumatized postwar Tokyo gave him pause for thought. In her, he believed, his showy, empty life found a sense of purpose.

Lennon left his wife and their stockbroker-belt country mansion and set up house with Yoko in a London flat. In 1968 they released *Unfinished Music #1: Two Virgins*, with a self-shot nude photograph of themselves on the cover. They married in March 1969 at the British Consulate in Gibraltar, and posed for the official photographs (taken by David Nutter) with John in a white suit and white turtleneck sweater and Yoko in a matching white minidress and high-domed floppy hat.

In the photo the couple are almost obscured by their own hair. Lennon and Ono represented a generation who were 'dropping out' all over America and Europe. The straggly hair and white suits reflected not only a change in fashion but a change in attitude. The love generation wanted more than the 50s ideals of regular pay cheques, a good car and a life in suburbia.

The couple promised to stage many 'happenings'. The first was the honeymoon 'bed-in' for peace in the Amsterdam Hilton. Then there was the huge billboard in Times Square, New York: 'WAR IS OVER—if you want it.' For the next decade, they took aim at stiff white-collar America. Lennon's fame mingled perfectly with Ono's bold performance art to create photogenic anti-war messages.

Four days after this picture was taken of the newlyweds at Heathrow Airport, John and Yoko were in Canada to launch another 'bed-in'. Having spent their honeymoon in bed in Amsterdam and the intervening weeks pursuing fruitless efforts to engage world leaders in peace talks, they headed across the Atlantic. Their all-white look has become an enduring symbol of New Age styling.

MARIANNE FAITHFULL

1969

The eternal rock chick as years go by

The daughter of a British military officer and a former ballerina, Marianne Faithfull was a teenager when she was first introduced to the court of the Rolling Stones in 1964. Jagger and Richards wrote 'As Tears Go By' for her, and the 17-year-old schoolgirl from Hampstead found herself transformed into a pop star. She was the inspiration for may Rolling Stones records, including 'Let's Spend the Night Together', 'You Can't Always Get What You Want' and 'Wild Horses', and she wrote the lyrics for 'Sister Morphine'.

With her wide-eyed look, long golden hair, flirty babydoll dresses and knee socks, Faithfull epitomized the style of the decade. She was a 1960s beauty who was also once memorably described as an 'angel with t—'. She also embodied the rock 'n' roll lifestyle.

Before she was 21 Faithfull had one marriage and a son behind her; she had rejected the advances of a love-struck Bob Dylan who dedicated poetry to her; had had brief affairs with both Brian Jones and then Keith Richards, who suggested that she and Mick Jagger would make a great couple. 'Go on, love, give him a jingle; he'll fall off his chair. He's not that bad when you get to know him', was Richards' advice to her.

When the police invaded the Stones' world in 1967 and found illegal pills that belonged to Faithfull, Jagger 'gallantly' accepted the blame. The London tabloids immortalized her in the headline 'Scantily Clad Woman at Drug Party'.

In the 1968 film *Girl on a Motorcycle,* Faithfull shocked audiences in a fur-lined leather jumpsuit. Her personal style effortlessly mixed rock 'n' roll style with hippie chic. You don't have to delve too deeply to figure out that the Faithfull repertoire is where Kate Moss has got some of her best ideas.

By her own admission, in an interview with the *New Musical Express*, Faithfull's 'first move was to get a Rolling Stone as a boyfriend. I slept with three and decided the lead singer was the best bet.' As venal as that sounds, she is nevertheless credited with serving as inspiration for much of Jagger's finest work.

SAFARI JACKET

The ultimate In utilitarian luxury

Three years after opening the Rive Gauche store for women on rue de Tournon, Yves Saint Laurent opened a menswear store on the same street. He was photographed by Helmut Newton at the opening party wearing a safari jacket.

It was the birth of another Saint Laurent icon. The four-pocket classic has been a staple of the YSL wardrobe ever since, alongside the tuxedo, the pant suit and the pea coat. Over more than 40 years it has been reinterpreted as menswear and as womenswear, as outerwear, as formal wear, as a laid-back tunic and as a seductive dress.

But in 1968 it belonged very much to the men's wardrobe, as characterized by the rugged machismo of Ernest Hemingway or the Afrika Korps. It may only have been a piece of clothing, but fashion's takeover and reinvention of this piece of utility kit perfectly symbolized the social and political tumult of the late 1960s, and further blurred the distinction between masculine and feminine.

Ironically, the first safari jacket was not made for a collection at all. It was made to order for an appearance in a safari-themed fashion story shot by Franco Rubartelli for French *Vogue* in 1968 and modelled by Veruschka, who strode across the bush with a hunting knife in her belt and a rifle across her shoulders. The shoot itself had been inspired by the runaway success that was Saint Laurent's African collection of 1967. *Harper's Bazaar* of March 1967 described the garments as 'a fantasy of primitive genius, shells and jungle jewellery, clustered to cover the bosom and hips, latticed to bare the midriff.'

Short, sexy, worn with a belt with a ring-shaped buckle, the Veruschka piece embodied the spirit of liberty that was shaking up wardrobes. In the wake of its success, production of the Saint Laurent safari jacket was started immediately, and it was sold in Rive Gauche boutiques the following season. There has barely been a YSL collection without some manifestation of the safari jacket ever since.

Since its first magazine appearance, the safari jacket has appeared in the guise of glossy evening glamour, as a sharply tailored City suit or as a laid-back companion to dressed-down denim. It may have started as a happy fashion accident, but the '*saharienne*' remains a classic that is as cool today as it ever was.

INDEX

Italic page numbers
indicate illustrations.

About Town magazine 12
air travel 52
America
    Bonnie and Clyde 64
    Kennedys 6, 20, 56, 68
    London Look 12, 38, 74
    Oleg Cassini 68
    psychedelia 78–9
    topless swimsuit 34–5
animal prints 90
Antonioni, Michelangelo
    14, 48, 92, 96
Arbus, Diane 76
Armani, Giorgio 72
ashram experience 82–3
Aspinall, Neil 82
Avedon, Richard 22, 54–5,
    76, 80

Bacall, Lauren 20, 56, 70
Bailey, David 12, 22, 32–3,
    48, 76
Baker, Caroline 50
Baldwin, Billy 20
Balenciaga, Cristóbal 22, 30
Barbie 52
Bardot, Brigitte 24, 46, *47*,
    66, 92, 96
Bassman, Lillian 54
Battele, Kenneth 20–1
Bazaar boutique 74
The Beatles 66, 82, *83*, 94
beautiful people 22
Beck, Jeff 48
Belmondo, Jean-Paul 10, *11*
Berenson, Marisa 22
Bergé, Pierre 58
Bergman, Jo 60
Birkin, Jane 48, 96, *97*
Birtwell, Celia 84–5
black dress 18
black and white 56–7, 76, 90
body painting 92
bohemian look 66, 96
Booker, Christopher 50

boutiques 58, 66, 74, 84
Boyd, Patti 46, *83*
bras 34, 98
Brodovitch, Alexey 54
Buñuel, Luis 62
Burberry 76

Capote, Truman 56–7, 76
Cardin, Pierre 24, 68
Cassini, Oleg 68
Chanel, 'Coco' 74, 100
Christie, Julie 42–3
cinema *see* films/cinema
Clarke, Ossie 66, 84–5
coats 16, 18, 42, *43*
Cohen, Sheila 66
communal living 78, 82
cosmetics 8, 40, 58, 98
Courrèges, André 22, 30–1
Cowan, John 48
Crosby, John 6

Daily Express 80
Daily Telegraph 6
Dalton, Phyllis 42
Deacon, Giles 92
Delon, Alain 44
Deneuve, Catherine 32,
    62–3, 70, 76
Donovan, Terence 48
dresses
    black evening 18
    glow-in-the-dark 30
    paper 38
    queen of the dress 100
    sheer 96
    straight-cut shift 74
    topless 34
drugs 78, 82, 94, 98, 104
Dunaway, Faye 64–5
Dylan, Bob 40, 78, 104

Echols, Alice 98
Ekberg, Anita *15*
Emerson, Gloria 70
Eurovision Song Contest 16
Evans, Walker 64

The Factory, New York 40
Fairchild, John 42
Faith, Adam 16
Faithful, Marianne 60, 104–5
Farrow, Mia 36, 56, *57*, 82
Fellini, Federico 14
films/cinema 6, 14
    Barbarella 60, 94
    Belle de Jour 62–3
    Billy Liar 42
    Blow-Up 32, 92, 96
    Bonnie and Clyde 64–5
    Breakfast at Tiffany's
        18–19, 56
    Breathless 10–11
    Cleopatra 28–9, 90
    Dr Zhivago 42, *43*
    Far from the Madding
        Crowd 42
    Funny Face 54
    Girl on a Motorcycle 104
    In Cold Blood 56
    Jules et Jim 24–5
    La Dolce Vita 14, 44
    Performance 60
    Rosemary's Baby 36, 56
    Saint Joan 10
    Scandal 26
    Slogan 96
    Vinyl 40
    Viva Maria! 24, 46
    The World of Suzie Wong
        36
Finnish fashion 72–3
flower power style 46, 78
Ford, Eileen 44

Gainsbourg, Serge 44, 96
Galliano, John 40
Garavani, Valentino 90–1
Gernreich, Rudi 34–5
Getty, Talitha 94–5
Givenchy, Hubert de 18, 68
Godard, Jean-Luc 6, 10, 14
Goldstein, Richard 98
Granny Takes a Trip 66–7
Grossman, Henry 56

hair styles
  afro 78, 86, *87*
  bobs 16, 36, 64
  bouffant 8, 20, 68
  long 78, 102
  romantic look 46
  short 10, 36, 80
hairdressers
  House of Leonard 80
  Kenneth Battelle 20–1, 56
  Vidal Sassoon 36–7
Hardy, Françoise 70, 96
Harper's Bazaar 22, 28, 52, 54, 106
hats 60–1, 64, 68, 102
hemlines
  maxi 42, *43*
  midi 64
  mini 12, 30, 42, 70, 96, 102
Hemmings, David 48, 92
Hendrix, Jimi 66, 78, 86, 94
Hepburn, Audrey 18–19, 20, 90
hippie style 78, 84, 94, 98
Hollywood 10, 14, 28–9
Hunt, Marsha 86, *87*

Isola, Maija 72
Italy
  Emilio Pucci 52
  La Dolce Vita 14, 44
  Missoni 88
  Valentino 90

jackets 58, 70, *71*, 106–7
Jacobs, Marc 22
Jagger, Mick 32, 60, 86, 104, *105*
Jane & Jane 100
jersey 100
Jones, Brian 44, 60, 104
Joplin, Janis 94, 98, *99*
journalism 14, 26, 50

Kampner, Nan 70
Kardashian, Kim 28
Kavanagh, Julie 94
Keeler, Christine 26–7

Kennedy, Jackie 6, 20, 52, 68–9, 72, 90
Khanh, Emmanuelle 88
Klein, William 22
knitwear 88–9
Kurtz, Irma 50
Kwan, Nancy 36

Lean, David 42
Lennon, John 76, 82, *83*, 102, *103*
Lerman, Leo 56
Lichfield, Patrick 86, 94
Life magazine 56, 58, 80
London
  Carnaby Street 66
  Jean Muir 100
  Kings Road 58, 66, 74
  Nova magazine 50
  op art fashion 38
  photography 6, 32, 48, 80
  Quorum boutique 84
  social changes 6, 26
London Look 12, 38, 74
Loren, Sophia 52, 90

Maharishi Mahesh Yogi 82–3
make up 8, 40, 58, 98
Marimekko 72–3
Marrakesh 94, *95*
Mastroianni, Marcello 14
Mayfair style 46
McCullin, Don 50
McSharry, Deirdre 80
midi skirt 64
Milan 88
military tailoring 42, 106
Miller, Sienna 40, 60
miniskirt 12, 30, 42, 70, 96, 102
Missoni, Ottavio 'Tai' 88–9
Mod fashion 8, 38, 60
models
  American *Vogue* 22, 54, 92
  black 58, 86
  Blow-Up 48, 92, 96
  Edie Sedgwick 40–1
  Jean Shrimpton 12
  Jeanne Moreau 24

Marsha Hunt 86, *87*
  Nico 44
  Penelope Tree *2*, 22, 76–7
  Twiggy 22, 54, 76, 80–1
  Veruschka 22, 48, 92, *93*
Moffit, Peggy 34
Monroe, Marylin 20, *21*, 52
moon girl look 30
Moreau, Jeanne 24–5, 46, *47*
Moss, Kate 40, 60, 104
Muir, Jean 100–1
Mulas, Ugo 92
Mulleavy, Kate and Laura 10
music
  ashram influence 82
  Dusty Springfield 8–9
  Jane Birkin 96
  Janis Joplin 94, 98, *99*
  John Lennon/Yoko Ono 102
  Marsha Hunt 86
  Nico 44
  psychedelia 78
  rock 'n' roll 50, 60, 104
  Sandie Shaw 16–17

Nemy, Enid 56
New Age style 102, *103*
New Musical Express 104
New York
  black and white ball 56, 76
  Diana Vreeland 22–3, 76
  Kenneth Battelle 20, 56
  Nico 44
  op art 38
  Penelope Tree 76
  The Factory 40, 60
  Twiggy 80
New York Times 14, 56, 70
New Yorker magazine 80
Newsweek magazine 80
Newton, Helmut 50, 80, 106
Nico 44–5
Nouvelle Vague 6, 24
Nova magazine 50–1
Nureyev, Rudolf 94
Nurmesniemi, Vuokko 72
Nutter, David 102

O'Brien, Mary 8
Ono, Yoko 102, *103*
op art 38–9

Page, Jimmy 48
Pallenberg, Anita 60–1, 66
Paris
  André Courrèges 22, 30–1
  Jean Seberg 10
  Jeanne Moreau 24
  Nico 44
  Valentino 90
  Yves Saint Laurent 58–9,
    62, 106–7
Parkin, Molly 50
peace movement 102
Pearse, John 66
Penn, Irving 22
Penney, J.C. 74
photography
  Blow-Up 48–9, 92
  David Bailey 32–3, 48
  Lichfield, Patrick 86, 94
  paparazzi 14
  Richard Avedon 54–5
Piaggi, Anna 88
Plunket Greene, A. 74
Pollock, Alice 84
pop art 6, 70
Premiere magazine 48
Preppy style 10
Profumo, John 26
psychedelia 38, 52, 66, 78–9
Pucci, Emilio 52–3
PVC 30

Quant, Mary 30, 36, 50,
  66, 74–5
Quorum boutique 84

radio 50, 96
Ratia, Armi 72
ready-to-wear fashion 58,
  74, 90, 100
red, Valentino 90
Richards, Keith 60, *61*, 104
Riley, Bridget 38–9
Rishikesh, India 82

Rive Gauche 58–9, 106
Rodarte label 10
Rolfe, Colin 12
The Rolling Stones 32, 44,
  60, 66, 86, 94, 104
romantic look 46–7, 84
Rome 14, 28, 60, 90
Roxon, Lillian 98
Rubartelli, Franco 92, 106

safari jacket 106–7
Saint Laurent, Yves 58–9,
  62, 94, 106–7
San Francisco 78, 98
Sant'Angelo, Giorgio di 92
Sassoon, Vidal 36–7
Seberg, Jean 10–11
Sedgwick, 'Edie' 40–1, 94
Sevigny, Chloë 44
sexual revolution 26, 50,
  78, 82
Shaw, Sandie 16–17
Shrimpton, Jean 12–13, 22
Sinatra, Frank 36, 56, *57*
Smith, Patti 40
Le Smoking 58, 70, *71*
social changes 6, 26, 50, 86
Sontag, Susan 50
Space Age look 22, 30–1
spirituality 78, 82, 102
sporting fashion 52, 88
Sports Illustrated 72
Springfield, Dusty 8–9
Stamp, Terence 12
suits 70–1, 106
Summer of Love 78
swimsuits 30, 34–5

tattoos 98
Taylor, Elizabeth 28–9, 90
television 50, 56
Time magazine 42, 66
Tree, Penelope 2, 22, 76–7
trousers
  bell-bottom 78
  Courrèges 30
  Emilio Pucci 52
  Nico 44, *45*

romantic look 46
  Yves Saint Laurent 58, 70
Truffaut, François 24
Twiggy 22, 54, 76, 80–1
Tynan, Kenneth 6

Valentino 90–1
Van Runkle, Theadora 64
vegetarianism 78, 82
Velvet Underground 44, *45*
Veruschka 22, 48, 92–3, 106
Vincendeau, Ginette 24
vintage clothes 66
Vogue
  André Courrèges 30
  David Bailey 32
  Diana Vreeland 22–3, 76
  Edie Sedgwick 40
  Jane Birkiln 96
  Jean Shrimpton 12
  Marsha Hunt 86
  new social order 6
  Richard Avedon 54
  romantic look 46
  safari jacket 106
  Twiggy 80
  Valentino 90
Volkswagen bus 78
Vreeland, Diana 22–3, 54,
  76, 80, 88, 92

Wadsworth, Derek 8
Ward, Stephen 26
Warhol, Andy 6, 40, 44,
  45, 60, 66
Watson, Linda 84
Watt, Judith 84
Waymouth, Nigel 66
Westminster, Duchess of 6
white 90, 102, *103*
The Who 38, 48, 86
Wolfe, Tom 32
Women's Wear Daily
  42, 68, 88
Wyndham, Frances 62

The Yardbirds 48
youth culture 6, 22, 26, 30, 50

PICTURE CREDITS

FURTHER READING

Breeland, Lisa I (2010),
*Diana Vreeland: The Eye
Has to Travel*, Abrams

Devlin, Polly (1979),
*Vogue Book of Fashion
Photography*,
Simon & Schuster

Duras, Marguerite (2010),
YSL: Icons of Fashion,
Schirmer/Mosel Verlag GmbH

Edkins, Diana and Tapert,
Annette (2005), *The Power
of Style*, Crown Publications

Howell, Geaorgina (1978),
*In Vogue: Sixty Decades of
Fashion*, Penguin Books Ltd

Jones, Dylan (1990), *Haircults*,
Thames & Hudson Ltd

Rennolds Millbank, Caroline
(1989), *New York Fashion:
The Evolution of American
Style*, Harry N. Abrams, Inc.

Taylor, Elizabeth (2002),
My Love Affair with Jewellery,
Simon & Schuster

Vreeland, Diana (2010),
Allure, Chronicle Books

CREDITS

First published in 2012
by Conran Octopus Ltd
a part of Octopus Publishing
Group, Endeavour House,
189 Shaftesbury Avenue,
London WC2H 8JY
www.octopusbooks.co.uk

An Hachette UK Company
www.hachette.co.uk

Distributed in the US by
Hachette Book Group USA,
237 Park Avenue, New York,
NY 10017 USA

Distributed in Canada by
Canadian Manda Group,
165 Dufferin Street, Toronto,
Ontario, Canada M6K 3H6

British Library Cataloguing-
in-Publication Data.
A catalogue record for this
book is available from the
British Library.

Text written by: Paula Reed

Publisher: Alison Starling
Consultant Editor:
Deyan Sudjic
Senior Editor: Sybella Stephens
Editor: Robert Anderson
Art Director: Jonathan Christie
Design: Untitled
Picture Research:
Anne-Marie Hoines
& Sara Rumens
Production: Caroline Alberti

ISBN: 978 1 84091 604 1
Printed in China